Beatrice Trum Hunter

THE FAMILY WHOLE GRAIN BAKING BOOK

BREADS • ROLLS • COOKIES • CONFECTIONS

Other Keats books by Beatrice Trum Hunter

BEATRICE TRUM HUNTER'S ADDITIVES BOOK

BREWER'S YEAST, WHEAT GERM, LECITHIN

GLUTEN INTOLERANCE

WHEAT, MILLET AND OTHER GRAINS

YOGURT, KEFIR AND OTHER MILK CULTURES

Beatrice Trum Hunter

THE FAMILY WHOLE GRAIN BAKING BOOK

BREADS • ROLLS • COOKIES • CONFECTIONS

KEATS PUBLISHING INC. NEW CANAAN, CONNECTICUT

To

adventurous cooks interested in good nutrition

THE FAMILY WHOLE GRAIN BAKING BOOK

Originally published under the title *Beatrice Trum Hunter's Baking Sampler*

Library of Congress Cataloging-in-Publication Data
Hunter, Beatrice Trum
The family whole grain baking book : breads, rolls, cookies,
confections / by Beatrice Trum Hunter.
p. cm.
Originally published: New Canaan, Conn. Keats Pub., 1972.
Includes index.
ISBN 0-87983-598-2 : $14.95
1. Baking. 2. Cookery (Cereals) I. Title.
TX765.H87 1993 92-38213
641.8'16—dc20 CIP

Printed in the United States of America
Published by Keats Publishing, Inc.
27 Pine Street (Box 876)
New Canaan, Connecticut 06840-0876

Contents

Breads and Rolls

Cookies and Confections

FOREWORD TO THE NEW EDITION

The values of whole grains and whole-grain flours have become better recognized for their contributions to good health. "The Eating Right Pyramid: A Guide to Daily Food Choices" launched by the U.S. Department of Agriculture, designates bread and other grain products at the base of the graphic pyramid. An average of six to 11 servings daily is recommended, and the use of whole-grain products is encouraged from this designated food group.

Formerly, dietary fibers were regarded merely as non-nutritive bulking agents that would prevent constipation. That over-simplified view has been replaced by a more sophisticated understanding of the vital roles played by different types of dietary fibers, both soluble and insoluble. It was learned that fibers may diminish the amount of cholesterol absorbed from food, as well as lower the amount of cholesterol that the body forms in the liver. Stools produced by a high-fiber diet tend to be bulkier and softer, and pass more quickly and easily through the intestine. Thus, any toxins or carcinogens present can be voided from the body before they have a chance to be absorbed.

The need for adequate intake of dietary fibers to maintain good health is due largely to the pioneering efforts of Dr. Denis P. Burkitt and his colleagues, Drs. Trowell and Cleave. Burkitt had observed that colon cancer, hemorrhoids, diverticular diseases, appendicitis, hiatal hernia, varicose veins, atherosclerosis, and ischemic heart diseases, were virtually unknown among Africans who lived in rural villages and ate high-fiber, low-fat, unrefined foods. These problems commonly afflict individuals in industrialized locations, where the diet is commonly low in fiber and high in fat, and consists mainly of refined foods. Then Burkitt noted that Africans who moved from their rural villages to urban areas, and began to eat the typical industrialized diet, soon developed similar health problems as those that plagued the industrialized populations.

Primarily through the studies and writings of Dr. Burkitt and his associates in the early 1970s, health professionals, scientific organizations, and governmental agencies responsible for health issues have come to a better appreciation of dietary fibers, and to recommend that adequate amounts be consumed. These fibers are supplied amply by many fruits and vegetables, and all whole grains.

Many whole grains and whole-grain flours have become familiar to shoppers in health food stores, and in specialty food shops and catalogs. In addition to the commonly recognized whole grains and whole-grain flours from wheat, rye, barley, oats, corn, buckwheat, and brown rice, others have been introduced to shoppers. They include millet, bulghur, amaranth, quinoa, spelt, teff, kamut, and triticale. Some of the more recently introduced whole grains and whole-grain flours have had long histories of use in other cultures. They are welcome. Many of these grains and flours can be substituted, partially or totally, for more commonly used ones. Some have an advantage for those who need to seek gluten-free grains and flours. They are especially appreciated by individuals who follow rotation diets in order to minimize food intolerances. All of the grains add greater variety to everyone's diet. Some experimentation may be necessary, because some lack the elasticity and binding property of gluten.

As many whole-grain food products have been introduced in the marketplace, what formerly had been appreciated only by a limited group now is widely enjoyed by the general population. No longer is any explanation of whole grains required. They have become familiar on Main Street, U.S.A.

Beatrice Trum Hunter, food editor
Consumers' Research Magazine
January 1993

NOTES FOR THE NOVICE

Revolt against plastic food in a plastic culture is in full swing, and commercial white bread has become the target for justified spoofing. It has been dubbed as "pre-sliced absorbent cotton," "cotton fluff wrapped up in a skin," and "pappy, tasteless, soft, aerated substances that are as appetizing as white foam rubber without the spring and the bounce." One writer commented that our bread is sliced, wrapped, steamed, and whitened to duplicate the consistency of old newspapers, with an unforgettable aroma of nothingness.

There is campus revolt, with students demanding "honest" whole-grain breads in the school cafeterias. There is supermarket revolt, with housewives demanding an end to overpriced deceptive "balloon bread" that is blown up to monstrous proportions. There is consumer revolt, with many concerned about the hazards of artificial emulsifiers, texturizers, stabilizers, dyes, mold retarders, and a host of other chemical adjuncts permitted in commercial baking. There is more consumer revolt, revealed when much of the bread served in restaurants, airplanes, hospitals, and other public places is rejected and ultimately finds its way to the pig farms.

"Who should make bread?" asked Sylvester Graham, that social critic whose name became associated with flour and crackers. In 1837, Graham demonstrated that neither the public bakers nor domestic servants had "those sensibilities and affections which alone can secure that careful attention, that soundness of judgment, that accuracy of operation, without which the best of bread cannot even uniformly, if ever, be produced."

With the flowery embellishments of the times, Graham concluded:

"It is the wife, the mother only—she who loves her husband and her children as women ought to love, and who rightly perceives the relations between the dietetic habits and physical and moral condition of her loved ones, and justly appreciates the importance of good bread to their physical and moral welfare—she alone it is, who will be ever inspired by that cordial and unremitting affection and solicitude which will excite the vigilance, secure the attention, and prompt the action requisite to success, and essential to the attainment of that maturity of judgment and skillfulness of operation, which are the indispensable attributes of a perfect breadmaker. And could wives and mothers fully comprehend the importance of good bread in relation to all the bodily and intellectual and moral interests of their husbands and children, and in relation to the domestic and social and civil welfare of mankind, and to their religious prosperity, both for time and eternity, they would estimate the art and duty of breadmaking far, very far more highly than they now do. They would then realize that, as no one can feel so deep and delicate an interest for their husbands' and children's happiness as they do, so no one can be so proper a person to prepare for them that portion of their aliment, which requires a degree of care and attention that can only spring from the lively affections and solicitude of a wife and mother."

Although Graham advised that the art of bread baking be returned to the wife and mother, today bread is being made by men as well as women, from teenagers to octogenarians. Many individuals have returned to the art of bread baking. Others approach it as novices. Many would bake bread, if only given a little encouragement and instruction. Thus, this sampler meets a need. All who make bread admit enthusiastically that bread baking is a creative, satisfying experience. It gets down to the essentials in life.

Only a few simple techniques need to be learned. Ingredients are readily available. No special equipment is necessary. Nor is breadmaking time-consuming. Some breads can be made, from start to finish, in less than two hours. There are breads that require no kneading—a practice long viewed as synonymous with drudgery.

While no *one* bread may satisfy all palates, there is variety enough for everyone to find some breads to his liking. The world seems to be divided into two groups: those who favor light-colored, feathery breads, contrasted to those who enjoy the dark-colored, dense ones. Perhaps it is habit. Perhaps it is social custom, of patricians versus plebeians. In this sampler, you will find breads both light and dark, spongy and hearty.

In general, I have eliminated from consideration those breads dependent on devitalized flours. The milling of wheat into refined white flour removes, among other nutrients:

60 per cent of the calcium
71 per cent of the phosphorus
85 per cent of the magnesium
77 per cent of the potassium
78 per cent of the sodium

In addition to these major elements, many trace elements also essential for life and health are removed:

40 per cent of the chromium
86 per cent of the manganese
76 per cent of the iron
89 per cent of the cobalt
68 per cent of the copper
78 per cent of the zinc
48 per cent of the molybdenum

In "enriched" flour, only the calcium and iron are put back, and the iron is added in a form poorly absorbed. Despite the "enrichment" program, the country continues to show signs of calcium and iron deficiencies.

In some recipes that follow, where white flour is used to a limited extent, it is *unbleached,* and fortified with the Triple Rich Cornell Formula, which adds wheat germ, soy flour, and nonfat dry milk powder. These three ingredients raise the nutritional standards of the flour, without radically changing either the taste or appearance of the finished baked product.

For many recipes, I have specified dry yeast granules, instead of compressed yeast cakes or packages of yeast. The yeast cakes, with limited shelf life, and requiring refrigeration, now contain an undesirable added antioxidant. The major cost of the dry yeast granules packed in individual packages consists mainly of the packaging material. For thrift, and to avoid the objectionable antioxidant, it is wise to purchase the dry yeast granules loose, by the pound, half pound, or quarter pound. The loose dry yeast granules are readily found in health food stores or through mail order companies. This yeast should be transferred to a tightly closed container. Stored in a cool, dry place, it will remain active, if unrefrigerated, for at least six months. For anyone who bakes regularly, buying the dry yeast granules in quantity assures a supply on hand for each baking.

One tablespoonful of the granules equals one package of dry yeast granules, or one cake of compressed yeast. One pound of dry yeast granules contains approximately forty-eight tablespoons. If you wish to convert a traditional recipe, and it calls for one ounce of yeast, use three tablespoons of the dry yeast granules.

For the beginning bread baker, the *only* crucial act in the entire procedure is at the beginning: softening the yeast. It is vital to have the water at the proper temperature in order to activate the yeast. The water should be *warm; not* hot; *not* lukewarm. Hot water will kill the yeast and inactivate it. Lukewarm water is too cool and fails to activate the yeast. If the mixture does not bubble within five to ten minutes after the yeast has been softened in the warm water, the water was probably too hot, or not warm enough. Start anew, with fresh yeast and water. Otherwise, you will waste precious bread ingredients and have bricklike loaves. If, on your second try, you have been careful to have the water at the proper temperature, but still fail to activate the yeast, assume that the yeast is too old and has become inactive. Replace it with fresh stock.

A small amount of sweetening added to the warm water and yeast will hasten the action of the yeast. However, be careful not to add *cold* honey or molasses in any quantity to the water-yeast mixture, or it will retard, rather than hasten the action. Potato water, which not only helps to keep bread moist, also hastens the rising.

If you are pressed for time during a baking session, use more baking yeast. If you double the amount, it will not affect the quality of the bread, and it will shorten the rising time.

Breads made with yeast keep fresh longer, and do not dry out as quickly as those made with baking powder. Yeast is rich in the B vitamins, while baking powders are B-vitamin destroyers.

In an attempt to substitute liquid vegetable oils for solid fats as much as possible in food preparation, I extended this procedure to bread baking as well. Not only is it healthier, by reducing the intake of saturated fats, but it is *easier.* It is far quicker to measure liquid oil than the cumbersome water-displacement or actual measurement of solid fats. Also, remember to measure the oil *before* you measure your honey, molasses, or other syrupy sweeteners. The cup, being coated with oil, will allow the sweetener to leave the cup readily. None gets wasted.

Which vegetable oils are suitable for bread baking? Any of the mild-flavored ones (corn, peanut, safflower, sesame, etc.) are good. Avoid the strong-flavored ones, which may be fine for salad dressing, or for brushing over fish to be baked, but will overpower baked products.

My own experience has been that the most satisfactory way of greasing bread pans and muffin pans is to use butter. Oil is less satisfactory for these utensils. It makes the baked products stick, and difficult to remove. On the other hand, cooky sheets, and mixing bowls for storing balls of dough while rising, are satisfactorily greased with oil.

Just as bleached, refined flours should be shunned because of their nutritional impoverishment, so should refined sugars be avoided. Fortunately, there are nutritionally rich natural sweeteners that can be substituted. Honey is perhaps the first choice, in popularity. Choose the light-flavored ones for baking (for example, clover) so that they do not predominate in the baked product. The dark-flavored ones (for example, buckwheat) are good on toast, waffles, etc.

Honey is especially favored for baking since it retains moisture. This keeps baked products from drying out.

Unsulfured molasses, stronger in flavor than honey, is excellent for certain types of baked products. Blackstrap molasses, nutritionally very rich, is somewhat bitter, and must be used sparingly. It is good in combination with unsulfured molasses or with honey.

What other natural sweeteners can be used? Maple syrup and maple sugar are delicate in flavor. Sorghum molasses, malt, and carob syrups all have distinctive flavors. They appear slightly less sweet than either honey or molasses.

There are still other natural sweeteners. Carob powder, malted-milk powder, whey powder, and nonfat dry milk powder all have a natural sweetness. The use of dried fruits, carrots, and squash can add sweetness to baked products, and allows the cook to cut down on other sweetening agents in the recipes.

For the beginning breadmaker, the entire procedure of

kneading seems like some skillful art. It really isn't! Here are a few hints. When the flour and liquid are well mixed in the bowl, and no longer stick to the sides, the dough is ready to be turned out and kneaded.

"How do you knead?" When a young woman asked me this question, I was stunned. But anyone knows how to knead! I began to mull it over. I grew up in an age when everyone's mother or grandmother made homemade bread. I learned how to knead by watching. Young people today may not have this opportunity. So, for those who have never seen anyone knead, this is the closest description I can give. Flour your fingers and palms and handle the dough lightly. Fold the edges of the dough toward the center, press down, and away, with your palms. Turn the dough over, and repeat. Continue doing this, quite rhythmically, until the dough is "smooth and elastic." You will know when the dough has reached this stage—which may take five minutes, eight minutes, ten minutes, or even fifteen minutes—when the dough no longer sticks to your hands or the board. If you press it with your finger, it will spring back into shape. Avoid overkneading, which may injure the baking quality of the gluten, and result in poor texture and volume. After you finish kneading, oil the surface of the dough. This will prevent it from drying out or cracking as it rises.

The gluten may also be injured if it is allowed to stand too long before being punched down. If the dough is allowed to rise too high in the pans before baking, it will result in coarse-grained bread. On the other hand, if you do not allow the dough to rise sufficiently in the pans before baking, your bread will be as heavy as a brick. All of this sounds more complicated than it is. A little experience will teach you how long to knead, and how long to allow the dough to rise.

How do you shape the dough for bread pan form? This is another question often asked. Divide your dough evenly into the number of loaves you intend to bake. Press, or roll, each piece into a flat, oblong piece. Take one long side, and fold one third of the dough over, and press it with the palm of your hand to seal. Then fold the other long side, overlapping the first. Press, and seal, as before. From the end, fold one third of the dough over. Press and seal. Fold the other end, overlapping the first. Press and seal. You have made an envelope. Now roll the sheet of dough lengthwise, like a jelly roll, making a round, compact loaf. Seal the overlap, and place the dough in a greased bread pan, with the overlap underneath.

The loaf should be half the depth of the pan. After the dough rises, the sides of the dough should be near the top of the pan, and the center should be well rounded.

Certain types of breads bake well when there is steam in the oven. You can place a pan of hot water on the bottom rack, while the bread is being baked.

If you like a shiny crust on bread, brush it with a beaten egg yolk, mixed with one tablespoon of cold water or milk, before you bake the bread. If you like to decorate your breads with seeds, brush the tops of the bread with this same mixture, before sprinkling the seeds on top. They will stay more securely in place. If you like hard-crusted breads, allow air to circulate around the loaves when they cool. If you enjoy soft-crusted breads, wrap the loaves in cloths while they are cooling. Or, you can brush the tops with melted butter, water, or milk, when you take the loaves out of the oven.

In most instances, quantities used in the following recipes yield more than a single loaf of bread. Usually pressed for time, I dislike wasting it. It is just as easy to make a few loaves of bread at one time as it is to make a single loaf. If you make a quantity beyond your own immediate needs, you will find that homemade bread is a much appreciated present to others. It also freezes well. If you have no friends (unlikely) or if you lack a freezer, you can always divide the recipe in half. If you think that you can't make a large batch because you lack the strength, think again. You can always mix a large amount in two bowls, or divide the dough in half, and knead each half individually. Some people have told me that they could not make homemade bread because they lacked large mixing bowls. What an excuse! A large enameled washbasin, a new scrubbing pail, or a vessel used for canning, all can double as mixing bowls.

If you plan to mix or knead stiff doughs, work at a low table in the kitchen, so that your arms are not bent awkwardly at a fatiguing angle. If you don't have a low table, try placing your mixing bowl in the bottom of the kitchen sink. If your bowl is too large to fit into the sink, instead of trying to lower the bowl, you can raise yourself. Place your bowl on the counter top, and you stand on a low footstool.

There is an elemental joy in baking bread. Many people like to get their hands into the dough. Perhaps we are still children playing with mud pies. Some persons especially enjoy working with yeast dough, which seems to have a life of its own, as it rises, falls, and rises again. I've even heard some exclaim as the bread comes out of the oven, "Such beautiful babies!" And who hasn't enjoyed the experience of various bread fragrances? The pungent aroma of fermented sourdough, the yeasty smell of the bread sponge, and the redolence wafting from the oven, as the bread is being baked? I shall say no more. Both author and reader are drooling.

Does homemade bread keep well? My husband's stock answer is, "No, not in this household. It's eaten up too quickly to spoil." Since homemade bread does not have the mold retarders of calcium or sodium propionate, used by most commercial bakers, it is best to keep bread refrigerated. This is especially true in hot, humid weather. Whole grain breads are more perishable than those made from refined flours. But even the whole grain ones will keep for one to two weeks, if refrigerated.

Many of the following recipes have free-form shapes of round loaves or long loaves, without the use of bread pans. There is a creative sense in "doing your own thing." You can form whatever shape you wish. You can decorate the tops of breads with seeds, pattern them with crisscross knife slashes, make them shine by brushing them with beaten egg yolk, or give them whatever other finishing touches you wish with your own special signature. Perhaps the free-form loaf is but another aspect of the revolt against the mechanization of life. The bread pans make for uniformity, the free form expresses a handiwork. Enough said. Begin to bake bread.

A Mini-Dictionary for the Bewildered Beginner

A MINI-DICTIONARY FOR THE BEWILDERED BEGINNER

arrowroot flour A natural thickening agent. It can be used as a substitute for white flour.

barley flour Unpearled or unpolished barley, ground finely.

bone meal A source of calcium. In powdered form, it can be added in limited quantity to baked goods.

brewer's yeast A non-leavening yeast and nutritional supplement. It is also known as "nutritional yeast," "primary yeast," or "food yeast." It is an excellent, inexpensive source of the vitamin B complex, and of protein. Because the taste is strong, begin with a small amount. Its flavor can be disguised in baked goods with a strong-flavored ingredient such as molasses.

carob powder Powder ground from the carob pod, which comes from a tree of the locust family. Toasted, carob powder strongly resembles chocolate, but it has none of chocolate's undesirable features. Whereas chocolate is high in fat, carob is not. For many people, chocolate is an allergen, especially for migraine-headache sufferers. Carob has no such adverse effects. Chocolate contains theobromine, a stimulant similar to caffeine; carob is free of stimulants. Carob is rich in minerals and natural sugars. Carob powder can be bought either plain or toasted. The latter more closely resembles chocolate in flavor. A great variation exists in the flavor of carob powder, as well as in its price. Some carob powders are more chocolate-like than others. A few are flat and disagreeably "gritty." If you do not find a palatable carob powder the first time you try, don't despair. Try another brand. Keep experimenting until you find the one you like. Carob powder is also sold as "carob flour." Flour is a misnomer, since it is not a flour in the sense that grain flours are. Instead, it is finely ground carob pods. Carob is also known as "St. John's bread," "honey locust," "locust bean," and "Boecksur."

carob syrup A natural sweetener, condensed from carob. (See above.)

corn flour Finely ground, undegerminated yellow corn.

cornmeal Coarsely ground, undegerminated yellow corn.

date sugar A natural sugar, made from dried ground dates. It resembles brown sugar in appearance, and if not kept moist, will cake in the same way.

gluten flour An elastic substance, found mainly in wheat and rye flours, that gives adhesiveness to dough. It is formed when the proteins in flour absorb water. Gluten coagulates when heated, and thus helps to give shape to baked bread. It is high in protein and devoid of starch. However, some people are allergic to gluten.

graham flour A wholewheat flour, with some of the bran removed.

kelp A seaweed, which can be obtained in powdered form. It is rich in minerals, vitamins, and trace elements. It can be used as a seasoning, as well as a nutritional supplement.

malt syrup A natural sweetener, made usually from germinated barley.

maple sugar Maple syrup, processed until it granulates.

meal A coarse flour, such as cornmeal or rye meal.

millet flour Millet, a whole grain, ground finely.

molasses, blackstrap A bitter syrup, made from sugar cane. Use sparingly.

molasses, unsulfured A sweet dark sugar cane syrup, 100% pure.

peanut flour Peanuts, ground finely. It is a rich source of protein, and can be added to grain flour. It will make the baked product dark and heavy.

potato flour A natural thickening agent. It can be used as a substitute for white flour.

rice flour Unpolished brown rice, ground finely.

rind, from organic fruit Rind that contains no dyes, waxes, fumigants, or pesticides.

rose hip powder The fruit of the rose, dried and pulverized. It is extremely high in vitamin C, and can be added in limited quantity to baked goods.

rye flour Whole grain rye, finely ground.

rye meal Whole grain rye, coarsely ground.

sea salt An unrefined salt, containing many minerals. Its source is the sea. It tastes the same as common table salt, sodium chloride.

sesame seed meal Sesame seeds, coarsely ground.

sorghum syrup A natural sweetener, made from a grain that is grown like corn.

soy flour Soybeans, ground finely. It is a rich source of protein, and can be added to grain flour. It is available as a full-fat soy flour, which is produced from the whole soybean, and is for general-purpose cooking; minimum-fat soy flour, which is good for making soy milk; and low-fat soy flour, which is good for baking. Soy flour makes the baked product brown and heavy. Baked goods containing soy flour should be baked at an oven heat 25% lower than usual.

soy grits A soybean product; its texture is similar to ground-up nuts.

soy lecithin Granules, made from defatted soybeans. They are a natural emulsifier, giving a smooth texture to baked goods. They can be used also as a nutritional supplement, for they are a rich source of phosphatides. The granules are also called "soy phosphatides."

sunflower seed meal Sunflower seeds, coarsely ground.

tahini A paste made from finely ground sesame seeds, in the same way that peanut butter is made from finely ground peanuts.

wheat germ The germ of the wholewheat berry.

whey powder Immortalized by Little Miss Muffet, this name for the watery part of milk is familiar to everyone. Whey contains milk sugar, minerals, and lactalbumin. In powder form, it serves as a nutritious supplement in baked goods.

Breads

LIGHT AND DARK, FLUFFY AND DENSE

BEATRICE TRUM HUNTER'S FAMOUS NO-KNEAD WHOLEWHEAT BREAD

This is a recipe that has undergone many modifications through the years, as I demonstrate bread baking before countless numbers of groups throughout the entire Northeast. Following Thoreau's famous dictum of "Simplify, simplify, simplify!" I have tried to get down to basics: a quick, effortless, foolproof, palatable, and nutritious bread that anyone can make. My husband says of this loaf, "Anyone can make it, including the village idiot."

1 tablespoon dry yeast granules
6 cups warm water (about)
2 tablespoons honey
14 cups wholewheat flour (unsifted)
1 tablespoon sea salt or kelp

Soften the yeast in 3 cups of the water, with the honey added. When this mixture bubbles, add it to the flour and salt (or kelp) in a large mixing bowl. Add the remaining 3 cups of water. Mix with your hands. The sole objective is to blend all the ingredients thoroughly and to get the dough the consistency of modeling clay. If the dough is too stiff, add more water, being careful not to add too much; if too thin, add more flour. Again, be careful not to add too much. When it has the right consistency, pat it down to the bottom of the bowl you have been mixing it in. Oil the surface of the dough. Cover, and set it in a warm place to allow it to rise until double in bulk (2 to 3 hours). Turn the dough out onto an *unfloured* board, and shape into 6 small loaves or 4 large loaves. Dip your fingers in cold water before shaping each loaf. Place the loaves in greased bread pans, and then place immediately in a *cold* oven. When all the bread pans are in the oven, set the oven control at 325° F. Bake the loaves for 50 to 60 minutes, depending on their size. No kneading, no punching down, no work, but 4 to 6 savory loaves of bread with a minimum of effort.

ALL-WHEAT BREAD

1 tablespoon dry yeast granules
1½ cups warm water
¼ cup honey
¼ cup oil
1½ cups milk
2 teaspoons sea salt or kelp
7 cups wholewheat flour (about)

Soften the yeast in the warm water, with the honey added. When the mixture bubbles, add the oil, milk, and salt (or kelp). Then add as much wholewheat flour as needed to make a moderately stiff dough. Turn out onto a lightly floured board, and knead until smooth and elastic. Shape dough into a ball, place it in a greased bowl, and brush the top with oil. Cover, and set in a warm place to rise until double in bulk. Divide the dough in half, and shape into 2 loaves. Place in 2 greased bread pans. Brush with oil, and cover. Let rise until double in bulk. Bake at 350° F. for 50 to 60 minutes. Yields 2 loaves.

NORWEGIAN WHEAT BREAD

2 cups water
$\frac{1}{4}$ cup honey
$\frac{1}{4}$ cup blackstrap molasses
$\frac{1}{2}$ cup oil
2 teaspoons sea salt or kelp
1 tablespoon dry yeast granules
$\frac{1}{2}$ cup nonfat dry milk powder
$\frac{1}{2}$ cup soy flour
$\frac{1}{2}$ cup wheat germ
2 cups wholewheat flour
2 to 3 cups unbleached white flour (about)

Mix in a saucepan 1$\frac{3}{4}$ cups of the water with the honey, molasses, oil and salt (or kelp). Bring to a boil and cool to lukewarm. While this mixture is cooling, soften the yeast in $\frac{1}{4}$ cup warm water. When the yeast mixture bubbles, add the cooked and cooled mixture. Add next the milk powder, soy flour, wheat germ, and wholewheat flour. Then add enough unbleached white flour to make a fairly stiff dough. Knead until the dough is smooth and elastic. Shape into a ball, and place in a greased bowl. Oil the top of the dough. Cover, and set in a warm place to rise until double in bulk. Punch down, and knead again. Shape into 2 loaves, and place in 2 greased bread pans. Allow to rise until double in bulk. Bake at 400° F. for 20 minutes, and then at 350° F. for 35 to 40 minutes longer. Yields 2 loaves.

WHOLEWHEAT POPPY-SEED BREAD

2 tablespoons dry yeast granules
4 cups warm water
½ cup honey
¼ cup blackstrap molasses
5 tablespoons oil
1 tablespoon sea salt or kelp
12 cups wholewheat flour (about)
½ cup poppy seeds

Soften the yeast in ½ cup warm water, with the honey and molasses added. When the mixture bubbles, add the rest of the water, oil, and salt (or kelp). Then add enough flour to make a moderately stiff dough. Turn the dough out onto a lightly floured board, and knead until it is smooth and elastic. Shape the dough into a ball, and place in a greased bowl. Brush the top with oil. Cover, and set in a warm place to rise until double in bulk. Punch down, and shape into 3 balls. Place the balls on greased cooky sheets, brush the tops with oil, and sprinkle with poppy seeds. Cover, and let rise again until double in bulk. Bake at 350° F. for 35 to 40 minutes. Yields 3 round loaves.

WHEAT-OAT BREAD

1 tablespoon dry yeast granules
2 cups warm milk
½ cup honey
½ cup oil
1 egg, beaten
1 teaspoon sea salt or kelp
3 cups wholewheat flour
3 cups oat flour (about)

Soften the yeast in ½ cup of the milk, with the honey added. When the mixture bubbles, add the oil, egg, the rest of the milk, and the salt (or kelp). Stir in the wholewheat flour. Then add the oat flour, using enough to make a moderately stiff dough. Turn out onto a lightly floured board, and knead for 10 minutes, or until smooth and elastic. Shape the dough into a ball, and place it in a greased bowl. Brush the top with oil. Cover, and set in a warm place to rise until double in bulk. Punch down, and shape into 3 loaves. Place in 3 greased bread pans. Let rise again until double in bulk. Bake at 375° F. for 45 to 50 minutes. Yields 3 loaves.

WHOLEWHEAT-RICE BREAD

2 tablespoons dry yeast granules
2½ cups warm water
½ cup honey
¼ cup oil
1 tablespoon sea salt or kelp
2 cups rice flour
1 cup soy flour
5 cups wholewheat flour (about)

Soften the yeast in the warm water, with the honey added. When the yeast mixture bubbles, add the oil, salt (or kelp), rice flour, and soy flour. Then add enough wholewheat flour to make a stiff dough. Roll into a ball, and place in a greased bowl. Oil the top of the dough. Cover, and set in a warm place to allow it to rise until double in bulk. Turn out onto a floured board, knead until smooth and elastic, and divide into 2 balls. Shape the balls into loaves, and place in greased bread pans. Cover, and set in a warm place to rise until double in bulk. Bake at 400° F. for 15 minutes, and then at 350° F. for 30 to 40 minutes longer. Yields 2 loaves.

WHOLEWHEAT-SESAME BREAD

2 tablespoons dry yeast granules
3½ cups warm water
⅓ cup honey
2 tablespoons sorghum syrup
1 tablespoon blackstrap molasses
2 tablespoons oil
¾ cup nonfat dry milk powder
1 tablespoon sea salt or kelp
1 tablespoon bone meal
½ cup soy flour
6 cups wholewheat flour (about)
⅓ cup sesame seeds

Soften the yeast in the warm water, with the 3 sweeteners added. When the yeast mixture bubbles, add the oil, milk powder, salt (or kelp), bone meal, and soy flour. Then add enough wholewheat flour to make a moderately stiff dough. Turn out onto a lightly floured board, and knead until smooth and elastic. Shape the dough into 3 balls of equal size, and place on greased cooky sheets. Brush the tops with oil, and sprinkle sesame seeds over them. Allow to rise until light, about 35 minutes. Bake at 350° F. for 30 to 35 minutes. Yields 3 round loaves.

WHEAT-OAT-BARLEY BREAD

1 tablespoon dry yeast granules
½ cup warm water
½ cup honey
½ cup oil
1 egg
6 tablespoons nonfat dry milk powder
6 tablespoons brewer's yeast
6 tablespoons soy flour
6 tablespoons wheat germ
2 teaspoons sea salt or kelp
1 cup oat flour
1 cup barley flour
4 cups wholewheat flour (about)

Soften the yeast in the water, with the honey added. When the yeast mixture bubbles, add the oil, egg, milk powder, brewer's yeast, soy flour, wheat germ, salt (or kelp), oat flour, and barley flour. Then add enough wholewheat flour to make a stiff dough. Turn the dough out onto a lightly floured board, and knead until it is smooth and elastic. Shape the dough into a ball, and place it in a greased bowl. Brush the top with oil. Cover, and set in a warm place to rise until double in bulk. Turn the dough out onto the floured board, punch down, and knead lightly. Shape into 3 loaves, and place in greased bread pans. Let the loaves rise in a warm place until nearly double in bulk. Bake at 400° F. for 10 minutes; then reduce the heat to 325° F. and bake for 15 to 20 minutes longer. Yields 3 loaves.

WHEAT GERM BREAD

1 tablespoon dry yeast granules
½ cup warm water
2 tablespoons honey
1 tablespoon unsulfured molasses
2 tablespoons oil
1 egg, beaten
2 cups milk
2 teaspoons sea salt or kelp
2 cups wheat germ
4½ cups wholewheat flour (about)

Soften the yeast in the water, with the honey and molasses added. When the mixture bubbles, add the oil, egg, milk, salt (or kelp), and wheat germ. Then add enough wholewheat flour to make a stiff dough. Turn the dough out onto a lightly floured board, and knead until it is smooth and elastic. Shape the dough into a ball, and place it in a greased bowl. Brush the top with oil. Cover, and set in a warm place for 1 hour. Then knead it again, lightly, and shape into 2 loaves. Place in 2 greased bread pans. Let the loaves rise in a warm place until double in bulk. Bake at 400° F. for 40 to 45 minutes. Yields 2 loaves.

ALL-GLUTEN BREAD

2 tablespoons dry yeast granules
2¼ cups warm water
1 tablespoon honey
1 teaspoon sea salt or kelp
4⅔ cups gluten flour (about)

Soften the yeast in the water, with the honey added. When the mixture bubbles, add the salt (or kelp). Then add enough gluten flour to make a moderately stiff dough. Turn the dough out onto a floured board, and knead for 10 to 15 minutes. Shape into 2 loaves, and place in greased bread pans. Cover, and set in a warm place to rise until double in bulk. Bake at 350° F. for 45 to 55 minutes. Yields 2 loaves.

ENRICHED ALL-GLUTEN BREAD

1 tablespoon dry yeast granules
3 cups warm milk
2 tablespoons honey
6 cups gluten flour (about)
1 egg
2 tablespoons oil
½ teaspoon sea salt or kelp

Soften the yeast in the milk, with the honey added. When the yeast mixture bubbles, add 1 cup of the gluten flour. Beat the mixture, and cover. Set in a warm place, and allow this sponge to rise. When it is light, add the egg, oil, and salt (or kelp). Then add enough of the remaining flour to make a moderately stiff dough. Turn the dough out onto a floured board, and knead until smooth and elastic. Shape into 2 loaves, and place in greased bread pans. Set in a warm place, and allow to rise again. Bake at 350° F. for 50 to 60 minutes. Yields 2 loaves.

GLUTEN-OATMEAL BREAD

2¼ cups water
2 cups rolled oats, uncooked
2 tablespoons dry yeast granules
½ cup unsulfured molasses
1 tablespoon oil
½ cup nonfat dry milk powder
½ cup soy flour
½ cup wheat germ
1 teaspoon sea salt or kelp
½ cup gluten flour
5 cups unbleached white flour (about)

Heat 2 cups of water to the boiling point, and pour over the rolled oats. Allow this mixture to cool to lukewarm. Soften the yeast in ¼ cup of warm water, with the molasses added. When the yeast mixture bubbles, combine it with the lukewarm rolled oats. Add the oil, milk powder, soy flour, wheat germ, salt (or kelp) and gluten flour. Then add enough unbleached white flour to make a moderately stiff dough. Knead the dough until it is smooth and elastic. Shape it into a ball, place in a greased bowl, and oil the top. Cover, and set in a warm place to rise until double in bulk. Punch down, knead lightly, and allow to rise again until double in bulk. Punch down again, shape into 2 loaves, and place in greased bread pans. Cover the loaves with a damp cloth, and allow to rise again. Bake at 350° F. for 55 to 60 minutes. Yields 2 loaves.

GLUTEN-SOY BREAD

1 tablespoon dry yeast granules
$2\frac{1}{4}$ cups water
1 teaspoon unsulfured molasses
1 tablespoon oil
1 teaspoon sea salt or kelp
$\frac{1}{2}$ cup nonfat dry milk powder
1 cup gluten flour
2 cups soy flour
3 cups unbleached white flour (about)

Soften the yeast in $\frac{1}{4}$ cup of warm water, with the molasses added. When this mixture bubbles, add the remainder of the water, the oil, salt (or kelp), milk powder, gluten flour, and soy flour. Then add enough unbleached white flour to make a stiff dough. Turn out onto a floured board, and knead until smooth and elastic. Shape into a ball, place in a greased bowl, and oil the top. Cover, and set in a warm place to allow the dough to rise until double in bulk. Punch down, knead briefly, return to the bowl, and allow it to rise again until double in bulk. Shape into 2 loaves. Place the loaves in greased pans, cover, and allow to rise again. Bake at 350° F. for 50 to 60 minutes. Yields 2 loaves.

OATMEAL BREAD

1 tablespoon dry yeast granules
1¾ cups warm water
2 tablespoons honey
1 tablespoon vegetable oil
2 teaspoons sea salt or kelp
5 tablespoons nonfat dry milk powder
5 tablespoons wheat germ
5 tablespoons soy flour
1½ cups rolled oats, finely ground
4½ cups unbleached white flour (about)

Soften the yeast granules in the water with the honey. When it bubbles add the oil and salt. Mix the remaining dry ingredients together (milk powder, wheat germ, soy flour, rolled oats, and white flour), adding enough white flour to make a firm dough. Knead on a floured board until smooth and elastic. Shape into a ball, and place in a greased bowl. Brush the top of the dough with oil. Cover and set in a warm place. Allow to rise. Punch down, and knead again. Shape into 2 loaves. Place in 2 greased bread pans. Bake at 350° F. for 50 to 60 minutes. Yields 2 loaves.

OATMEAL-HONEY BREAD

1 cup rolled oats, uncooked
2 cups boiling water
2 tablespoons dry yeast granules
⅓ cup warm milk
½ cup honey
¼ cup oil
½ cup nonfat dry milk powder
2 teaspoons sea salt or kelp
6½ cups wholewheat flour (about)

Combine the oats and boiling water and allow the mixture to stand for 30 minutes. Then soften the yeast in the milk. When the yeast mixture bubbles, add the oats mixture and then the honey, oil, milk powder, and salt (or kelp). Then add enough wholewheat flour to make a moderately stiff dough. Turn the dough out onto a lightly floured board, and knead until it is smooth and elastic. Shape into a ball, and place in a greased bowl. Brush the top with oil. Cover, and set in a warm place to rise until double in bulk. Punch down, and knead again. Shape into 2 loaves, and place in 2 greased bread pans. Let rise for 10 minutes. Bake at 325° F. for 50 to 60 minutes. Yields 2 loaves.

MILLET BREAD

2 tablespoons dry yeast granules
2 cups warm water
⅓ cup sorghum syrup
⅓ cup oil
1 tablespoon sea salt or kelp
1½ cups millet flour
1 cup oat flour
¾ cup gluten flour
2½ cups wholewheat flour (about)

Soften the yeast in the water, with the sorghum syrup added. When this mixture bubbles, add the oil, salt (or kelp), millet flour, oat flour, and gluten flour. Then add enough wholewheat flour to make a moderately stiff dough. Turn the dough out onto a floured board, and knead until smooth and elastic. Place the ball of dough in a greased bowl, and oil the top. Cover, and set in a warm place to rise until double in bulk. Turn out again onto the floured board, and knead lightly. Return the dough to the greased bowl, cover, and allow to rise again until double in bulk. Punch down, divide in half, and shape into loaves. Place in greased bread pans. Cover, and allow to rise. Bake at 350° F. for 50 to 60 minutes. Yields 2 loaves.

MILLET-CARROT BREAD

1½ cups millet flour
¾ cup boiling water
1 cup carrots, raw and grated
1 tablespoon honey
3 tablespoons oil
1 teaspoon sea salt or kelp
3 egg yolks
3 tablespoons cold water
3 egg whites, stiffly beaten

Trickle the millet flour into the boiling water slowly, stirring constantly, until the mixture is smooth. Add the carrots, honey, oil, and salt (or kelp). Blend thoroughly. Mix the egg yolks with the cold water, and gradually add to the batter. Then fold in the stiffly beaten egg whites. Pour the batter into a warm, greased 8x8x2-inch pan. Bake at 350° F. for 40 to 45 minutes. Cut into 2x2-inch squares. Yields 16 squares.

ALL-BARLEY BREAD

2 tablespoons dry yeast granules
1 cup warm water
¼ cup honey
1 tablespoon oil
1 teaspoon sea salt or kelp
2½ cups barley flour (about)

Soften the yeast in the water. When it bubbles, add the honey, oil, and salt (or kelp). Then add enough barley flour to make a thick batter. Turn into 2 greased bread pans. Cover, and set in a warm place to rise until double in bulk. Bake at 375° F. for 25 to 30 minutes. Yields 2 loaves.

BARLEY-RYE BREAD

2 tablespoons dry yeast granules
1 cup warm water
¼ cup honey
3 tablespoons oil
½ teaspoon sea salt or kelp
6 cups barley flour
1⅓ cups rye flour
½ cup nonfat dry milk powder
8 egg whites, beaten stiffly

Soak the yeast in the water. When it bubbles, add the honey, oil, salt (or kelp), barley and rye flours, and milk powder. Then fold in the egg whites. Turn the batter into 2 greased bread pans. Cover, and set in a warm place to rise until double in bulk. Bake at 350° F. for 20 to 25 minutes. Yields 2 loaves.

UNLEAVENED BARLEY-WHOLEWHEAT BREAD

This dense, unsweetened bread is an adaptation from a Tibetan recipe.

4 cups barley flour
½ cup oil
8 cups wholewheat flour
1 tablespoon sea salt or kelp
¼ cup sunflower seeds
¾ cup sesame seeds
7 cups boiling water
¼ cup tahini

Pan roast the barley flour in half of the oil until the flour is darkened. Add to the wholewheat flour. Stir. Add to this mixture the salt (or kelp), sunflower and sesame seeds. Stir. Blend in the remaining oil. Mix thoroughly by rubbing the flour between the palms of the hands. Add the boiling water, and mix. Add the tahini, and mix. Allow the mixture to cool for 15 minutes. Then turn it out onto a floured board, and knead. Divide the dough into 2 portions. Press the portions into 2 warm, greased bread pans. Using a sharp knife, cut a slit ½-inch deep lengthwise down the top of each portion of dough. Set the pans in a warm place for 6 hours, or overnight. Bake at 450° F. for 40 to 50 minutes. Yields 2 loaves.

RICE-RYE BREAD

2 tablespoons dry yeast granules
1 cup warm water
½ cup honey
½ cup oil
2 eggs
½ teaspoon sea salt or kelp
3 cups rye flour
1 cup rice flour (about)

Soften the yeast in the water. When it bubbles, add the honey, oil, eggs, salt (or kelp), and rye flour. Then add enough rice flour to make a soft dough. Turn out onto a floured board, and knead until smooth and elastic. Shape the dough into a ball, place in a greased bowl, and oil the top. Cover, and refrigerate for at least 8 hours. Shape the dough into 2 balls, and place on greased cooky sheets. Set in a warm place to rise, for at least 4 hours. Bake at 325° F. for 45 to 50 minutes. Yields 2 round loaves.

MIXED GRAINS BREAD

1 cup rolled oats, uncooked
2½ cups boiling water
2 tablespoons dry yeast granules
½ cup unsulfured molasses
3 tablespoons oil
1 tablespoon sea salt or kelp
½ cup gluten flour
½ cup wheat germ
2 cups wholewheat flour
½ cup sunflower seed meal
2½ cups unbleached white flour (about)

Stir the rolled oats into 2 cups of the boiling water, and let the mixture cool until lukewarm. Cool the remaining ½ cup of water to lukewarm, and soak the yeast in it. When the yeast mixture bubbles, add the oats mixture to it. Then add the molasses, oil, salt (or kelp), gluten flour, wheat germ, wholewheat flour, and sunflower seed meal. Finally, add enough unbleached white flour to make a stiff dough. Turn the dough out onto a floured board, and knead until smooth and elastic. Shape the dough into a ball, place in a greased bowl, and oil the top. Cover, and set in a warm place to rise until double in bulk. Turn out again onto the floured board, knead lightly, and return to the bowl. Cover, and allow to rise again. When double in bulk, punch down, and shape into 2 loaves. Place the loaves on greased cooky sheets, cover with a damp cloth, and allow to rise. Bake at 350° F. for 50 to 60 minutes. Yields 2 round loaves.

CORNMEAL BREAD

1 cup undegerminated yellow cornmeal
1 cup hot milk
½ cup hot water
3 egg yolks, beaten
¼ cup oil
1 tablespoon honey
1 teaspoon sea salt or kelp
¾ cup oat flour
3 egg whites, stiffly beaten

Blend the cornmeal with the milk, and allow the mixture to stand until it thickens. Slowly add the hot water to the beaten egg yolks, stirring until the mixture is thick and smooth. Add to the egg mixture the oil, honey, salt (or kelp), and oat flour. Fold in the cornmeal mixture. Then fold in the stiffly beaten egg whites. Turn into a greased 8x8x2-inch pan. Bake at 400° F. for 15 to 20 minutes, or until lightly browned. Cut into 2x2-inch squares. Yields 16 squares.

LEAVENED CORNMEAL BREAD

½ tablespoon dry yeast granules
1 cup warm water
1 tablespoon unsulfured molasses
¼ cup oil
¼ cup nonfat dry-milk powder
¼ teaspoon salt
¾ cup undegerminated yellow cornmeal
½ cup oat flour
¼ cup rice flour

Soften the yeast in the water, with the molasses added. When the yeast mixture bubbles, add the remaining ingredients and blend. Turn the batter into a greased 8x8x2-inch pan. Cover, and set in a warm place to rise until double in bulk. Bake at 375° F. for 25 to 30 minutes. Cut into 2x2-inch squares. Yields 16 squares.

CORNMEAL-WHOLEWHEAT SPOON BREAD

5 tablespoons oil
3 tablespoons honey
1 cup cold water
1 cup undegerminated yellow cornmeal
⅔ cup wholewheat flour
¼ cup nonfat dry milk powder
1 teaspoon sea salt or kelp

Beat together the oil, honey, and water until the mixture is light and creamy. Mix together the cornmeal, wholewheat flour, milk powder, and salt (or kelp). Then blend this dry mixture with the creamy one. Turn the batter into a greased 8x8x2-inch pan. Bake at 400° F. for 30 to 35 minutes. Cut into 2x2-inch squares. Yields 16 squares.

CORNMEAL-MILLET BREAD

½ cup undegerminated yellow cornmeal
1 cup milk
3 egg yolks
2 tablespoons water
1 tablespoon oil
½ teaspoon sea salt or kelp
¼ cup millet flour
3 egg whites, stiffly beaten

Combine the cornmeal and milk in a saucepan, and cook over low heat, stirring constantly, until the mixture thickens. Remove from the heat, and cool to lukewarm. Blend the egg yolks with the water, oil, and salt (or kelp). Add to this mixture the millet flour, and then combine with the cornmeal mush. Fold in the stiffly beaten egg whites, and turn the batter into a greased 8x8x2-inch pan. Bake at 325° F. for 40 to 45 minutes. Cut into 2x2-inch squares. Yields 16 squares.

CARROT-CORNMEAL BREAD

1 cup undegerminated yellow cornmeal
1 cup raw carrots, grated
1 tablespoon honey
2 tablespoons oil
1 teaspoon sea salt or kelp
¾ cup boiling water
2 egg yolks, beaten
2 tablespoons cold water
2 egg whites, stiffly beaten

Mix together the cornmeal, carrots, honey, oil, and salt (or kelp). Pour the boiling water over this mixture, blend, and allow to cool to lukewarm. Blend the beaten egg yolks with the cold water. Gradually add this mixture to the first. Then fold in the stiffly beaten egg whites. Pour the batter into a greased 8x8x2-inch pan. Bake at 400° F. for 20 to 25 minutes. Cut into 2x2-inch squares. Yields 16 squares.

ALL-SOY SPOON BREAD

3 cups milk
$1\frac{1}{2}$ tablespoons oil
1 teaspoon sea salt or kelp
$\frac{3}{4}$ cup soy flour
3 egg yolks, well beaten
3 egg whites, stiffly beaten

Scald 2 cups of the milk, and add to it the oil and salt (or kelp). Stir the remaining 1 cup of milk (cold) into the soy flour. Combine the two mixtures. Cook for 5 minutes over direct heat, stirring constantly. Cool slightly. Stir slowly into the well-beaten egg yolks. Fold in the stiffly beaten egg whites. Turn into a greased 12-well muffin pan. Bake at 375° F. for 25 to 30 minutes. Yields 12 muffin-size servings of spoon bread.

BANNOCK

Bannock is a New England version of cornmeal bread.

2 cups milk
½ teaspoon sea salt or kelp
¾ cup undegerminated yellow cornmeal
1 tablespoon oil
3 egg yolks, well beaten
3 egg whites, stiffly beaten

Combine the milk, salt (or kelp), cornmeal, and oil in the top of a double boiler. Cook the mixture over water, stirring constantly, until it thickens. Remove from the heat, and cool. Then add the well-beaten egg yolks, and beat. Fold in the stiffly beaten egg whites, and turn the batter into an 8x8x2-inch pan. Bake at 400° F. for 30 minutes. Cut into 2x2-inch squares. Yields 16 squares.

SPOON BREAD

1 cup undegerminated yellow cornmeal
2 cups cold water
2 teaspoons sea salt or kelp
1 cup milk
3 eggs
2 tablespoons oil

Mix the cornmeal, water, and salt (or kelp) in a saucepan. Boil for 5 minutes, stirring constantly. Remove from the heat, slowly add the remaining ingredients, and blend thoroughly. Turn into a well-greased 8x8x2-inch pan. Bake at 400° F. for 45 to 50 minutes. Cut into 2x2-inch squares. Yields 16 squares.

SOUTHERN SPOON BREAD

2 cups milk
¾ cup undegerminated yellow cornmeal
3 tablespoons oil
1 teaspoon sea salt or kelp
1 teaspoon honey
2 egg yolks, beaten
2 egg whites, stiffly beaten

Scald the milk in the top of a double boiler, over hot water. Gradually add the cornmeal to the scalded milk, stirring constantly. Add the oil, salt (or kelp), and honey. Mix thoroughly. Remove the mixture from the heat, and gradually add it to the beaten egg yolks. Mix well. Fold in the stiffly beaten egg whites. Turn the batter into a greased 1½-quart casserole. Set this in a pan of hot water. Bake at 400° F. for 50 to 55 minutes. Yields 4 to 6 servings.

ANADAMA BREAD

½ cup undegerminated yellow cornmeal
2 cups boiling water
2 tablespoons oil
½ cup unsulfured molasses
1 teaspoon sea salt or kelp
1 tablespoon dry yeast granules
½ cup warm water
5 cups oat flour (about)

Stir the cornmeal very slowly into the boiling water, and cook 5 minutes. Remove from the heat, and add the oil, molasses, and salt (or kelp). Cool to lukewarm. Soften the yeast in the warm water. When it bubbles, add it to the cooled cornmeal mixture. Then add enough oat flour to make a moderately stiff dough. Turn the dough out onto a lightly floured board, and knead until smooth and elastic. Shape into 2 loaves, place in greased bread pans, and let rise until light. Bake at 400° F. for 50 to 60 minutes. Yields 2 loaves.

WHEATLESS CORNBREAD

2 tablespoons dry yeast granules
4½ cups warm water
⅓ cup honey
⅓ cup oil
1 teaspoon sea salt or kelp
2 cups undegerminated yellow cornmeal
1 cup potato flour
1 cup rice flour

Soften the yeast in the water, with the honey added. When the yeast mixture bubbles, add the remainder of the ingredients, and blend. Pour the batter into 2 greased bread pans. Cover, and set in a warm place to rise until double in bulk. Bake at 350° F. for 25 to 30 minutes. Yields 2 loaves.

ALL-RYE BREAD

2 tablespoons dry yeast granules
4 cups warm water
1 tablespoon unsulfured molasses
1 tablespoon sea salt or kelp
1 tablespoon caraway seeds
11 cups rye flour (about)

Soften the yeast in the warm water, with the molasses added. When the yeast mixture bubbles, add the salt (or kelp), caraway seeds, and 4 cups of the rye flour. Beat into a smooth dough. Let the batter rise in the bowl in a warm place until double in bulk. Then add enough of the remaining flour to make a stiff dough. Turn onto a floured board, and knead. Divide the dough into 4 parts, shape into loaves, and place in 4 greased bread pans. Cover, and set in a warm place to rise until double in bulk. Brush the tops with cold water, and bake at 350° F. for 50 to 60 minutes. Yields 4 loaves.

RYE BREAD

1 tablespoon dry yeast granules
2 cups warm water
2 tablespoons unsulfured molasses
2 tablespoons oil
1 cup milk
1 teaspoon sea salt or kelp
1 tablespoon caraway seeds
3 tablespoons nonfat dry milk powder
3 tablespoons wheat germ
3 tablespoons soy flour
1½ cups unbleached white flour
5 cups rye flour (about)

Soften the yeast in the warm water, with the molasses added. When the yeast mixture bubbles, add the oil, milk, salt (or kelp), caraway seeds, milk powder, wheat germ, and the soy and white flours. Then add enough rye flour to make a stiff dough. Turn the dough onto a floured board, and knead until it is smooth and elastic. Shape into a ball, and place in a greased bowl. Brush the top with oil. Cover, and set in a warm place to rise until double in bulk. Divide into 2 parts, shape into loaves, and place in greased bread pans. Let rise again until double in bulk. Bake at 375° F. for 40 to 45 minutes. Yields 2 loaves.

24-HOUR RYE BREAD

1 tablespoon dry yeast granules
1 cup warm water
2 tablespoons oil
1 tablespoon sea salt or kelp
7 cups rye flour
additional warm water

Soften the yeast in 1 cup warm water. When it bubbles, add the oil, salt (or kelp), and 6 cups of the rye flour. Add enough additional warm water to make a soft dough. Beat the mixture with a spoon until it frees itself readily from the sides of the bowl. Cover the bowl, and set it in a cool place (45° to 55° F.) for 24 hours. Then, work in 1 more cup of rye flour. Knead, and shape into a ball. Place in a greased bowl, and oil the top. Cover, and place in a warm place, such as an oven between 85° and 95° F. Allow the dough to rise for a few hours. Punch down the dough, work out the air bubbles, and shape it into 2 loaves. Place in greased bread pans. Set the pans back into the warm place, covered with cloths, and allow the dough to rise 45 minutes longer. Bake at 325° F. for 1¼ to 1½ hours. Yields 2 loaves.

RYE-WHOLEWHEAT BREAD

1⅔ cups warm water
⅓ cup honey
3 tablespoons sorghum syrup
2 tablespoons blackstrap molasses
2 tablespoons oil
1 tablespoon caraway seeds
1 tablespoon dry yeast granules
2¾ cups wholewheat flour
1 tablespoon sea salt or kelp
3 cups rye flour (about)

Mix together in a saucepan 1 cup of water, the 3 sweeteners, oil, and caraway seeds. Bring this mixture to a boil, and cook for 3 minutes. Cool to lukewarm. Soften the yeast in the remaining ⅔ cup of warm water. When this mixture bubbles, add it to the cooled cooked mixture. Stir in the wholewheat flour, and beat until smooth. Cover, and set in a warm place to rise until double in bulk (about 45 minutes). Then add the salt (or kelp) and enough rye flour to make a stiff dough. Turn the dough out onto a floured board, and knead until smooth and elastic. Divide the dough in half, and shape into 2 balls. Place the balls on greased cooky sheets. Using a sharp knife, make several crisscross cuts on the tops of the balls of dough. Cover, and set in a warm place to rise until double in bulk. Bake at 350° F. for 30 to 35 minutes. Yields 2 round loaves.

RYE BREAD WITH ANISE SEEDS

1 tablespoon dry yeast granules
$2\frac{1}{4}$ cups warm water
1 tablespoon unsulfured molasses
1 tablespoon anise seeds
2 teaspoons sea salt or kelp
5 cups rye flour
4 cups unbleached white flour (about)

Soften the yeast in the water, with the molasses added. When the mixture bubbles, add the anise seeds, salt (or kelp) and rye flour. Then add enough white flour to make a stiff dough. Turn the dough out onto a floured board, and knead. Cover, and allow to rise on the board until double in bulk. Knead again, and shape into 3 round loaves. Place the loaves on greased cooky sheets, cover, and allow to rise until double in bulk. Bake at 450° F. for 10 minutes, and then at 325° F. 1 hour longer. Yields 3 round loaves.

Serve the bread sliced very thin.

SEEDED RYE BREAD

This is an adaptation of the limpe bread from Sweden.

2 cups water
⅓ cup unsulfured molasses
1 tablespoon sea salt or kelp
2 tablespoons caraway seeds, ground
2 tablespoons anise seeds, ground
2 tablespoons fennel seeds, ground
2 tablespoons dry yeast granules
⅓ cup grated orange rind, from organic fruit
½ cup gluten flour
2½ cups rye flour
3 cups wholewheat flour (about)

Mix in a saucepan, 1 cup of the water with the molasses, salt (or kelp), and seeds. Bring to a boil, and cook for 3 minutes. Cool to lukewarm. Soften the yeast in 1 cup of warm water. When it bubbles, combine with the cooked mixture. Add the orange rind, gluten flour, and rye flour. Mix well. Cover, and set in a warm place to rise until double in bulk. Then add enough wholewheat flour to make a stiff dough. Turn out onto a floured board, and knead. Place in a greased bowl, oil, cover, and set in a warm place to rise until doubled. Turn it out onto a floured board, and knead again. Return to the greased bowl, cover, and allow to double in bulk again. Punch down, knead lightly, and shape into 2 balls. Place the balls on greased cooky sheets, cover, and allow to rise until doubled. Bake at 350° F. for 45 minutes. Yields 2 round loaves.

WISCONSIN RYE BREAD

1 tablespoon dry yeast granules
1 quart warm water
2 cups potatoes cooked and pureed
1 tablespoon sea salt or kelp
8 cups rye flour
4 cups wholewheat flour (about)

Soften the yeast in ½ cup of water. When this mixture bubbles, add the rest of the water, the potatoes, sea salt (or kelp), caraway seeds and rye flour. Mix thoroughly. Then add enough wholewheat flour to make a stiff dough. Turn the dough out onto a lightly floured board and knead until smooth and elastic. Place in greased bowl, oil the top, cover, and set in a warm place to rise until double in bulk. Shape into two balls, oil again and place on greased cooky sheet. Set in warm place and allow to rise again. Bake at 375° F. for about 1 hour. Brush the tops with water after baking. Yields 2 round breads.

RYE-POTATO BREAD

1 tablespoon dry yeast granules
½ cup warm potato water
3 tablespoons honey
1 tablespoon oil
1 teaspoon sea salt or kelp
½ cup potatoes, cooked and mashed
2 cups rye flour
1 cup potato flour (about)

Soften the yeast in the potato water, with the honey added. When this mixture bubbles, add, in the order listed, the oil, salt (or kelp), potatoes, and rye flour. Then add enough potato flour to make a stiff dough. Turn the dough out onto a lightly floured board, and knead until smooth and elastic. Place in a greased bowl, oil the top, cover, and set in a warm place to rise until double in bulk (about 4 hours). Turn the dough out again onto the lightly floured board, knead, and shape into 2 balls. Place the balls on greased cooky sheets, cover with a damp cloth, and allow to rise. Bake at 450° F. for 10 minutes, and then at 350° F. for 40 to 50 minutes longer. Yields 2 round loaves.

BLACK BREAD—SCANDINAVIAN STYLE

This is the surbrod of Scandinavia.

1 tablespoon dry yeast granules
2¼ cups warm water
1 teaspoon unsulfured molasses
2 teaspoons sea salt or kelp
5 cups rye flour
1 tablespoon caraway seeds
4 cups unbleached white flour (about)
melted butter

Soften the yeast in the water, with the molasses added. When this mixture bubbles, add the salt (or kelp), rye flour, and caraway seeds. Then add enough unbleached white flour to make a stiff dough. Turn the dough out onto a floured board, and knead. Place in a greased bowl, and cover. Set in a warm place to rise until double in bulk. Knead again, and divide into 3 loaves. Place the loaves on greased cooky sheets, and let rise until double in bulk. Bake at 425° F. for 10 minutes, and then at 350° F. for about 1 hour. Brush the tops lightly with melted butter. Yields 3 round loaves.

BLACK BREAD—RUSSIAN STYLE

This is an adaptation of the peasant bread from Russia.

2 tablespoons dry yeast granules
2 cups warm water
½ cup unsulfured molasses
¼ cup oil
1 tablespoon sea salt or kelp
¼ cup carob powder
¼ cup gluten flour
2 cups rye flour
3¾ cups unbleached white flour (about)

Soften the yeast in the water, with the molasses added. When the yeast mixture bubbles, add the oil, salt (or kelp), and carob powder. Mix together thoroughly. Gradually add the gluten and rye flours. Then add enough unbleached white flour to make a stiff dough. Knead, form into a ball, place in a greased bowl, and oil the top. Cover, and set in a warm place to rise until double in bulk. Turn the dough out onto a floured board, and knead again. Return the dough to the bowl, cover, and allow to rise until double in bulk again. Shape into 2 balls, and place on greased cooky sheets. Cover with a cloth, and allow to rise until double in bulk. Bake at 350° F. for 50 to 60 minutes. Yields 2 round loaves.

BLACK BREAD–DANISH STYLE

This is the gammelsurbrod of Denmark.

½ tablespoon dry yeast granules
2 cups warm water
3¼ cups rye meal (about)
1 teaspoon sea salt or kelp
1¼ cups unbleached white flour (about)
melted butter

The night before baking this bread, "set the sponge." To do this, soften the yeast in the water until it bubbles, add 2 cups of the rye meal, and beat the mixture for 2 minutes. Cover, and set in a warm place to form a sponge by rising and falling, and souring. In the morning, beat the sponge. Then add the salt (or kelp), 1 additional cup of rye meal, and 1 cup of unbleached white flour. Beat the mixture for 3 minutes. Cover, and let rise until light and spongy. Punch down, and turn onto a board sprinkled with about ¼ cup each of rye meal and unbleached white flour. Knead, working in as much meal and flour as necessary for a stiff dough. When the dough is smooth and elastic, shape into 2 balls. Place the balls on greased cooky sheets, and cover with slightly dampened cloths. Let rise in a warm place until the surfaces begin to crack. Bake at 300° F. for about 1¼ hours. If you don't wish to have the loaves become hard and crusted on the bottom, place a shallow pan of hot water on the lowest rack of the oven while the bread is baking. When the breads finish baking, brush the tops with melted butter. Yields 2 round loaves. Serve the bread sliced very thin.

BLACK BREAD—GERMAN STYLE

This is the schwartzbrot of Germany.

3 tablespoons dry yeast granules
2 cups warm milk
6 cups rye flour
1 teaspoon sea salt
1 tablespoon unsulfured molasses
1 teaspoon caraway seeds

Soften the yeast in ½ cup of the milk. When this mixture bubbles, add 2 cups of the rye flour, and blend thoroughly. Then set aside to rise and form a sponge. Stir the salt and molasses into the remainder of the milk. Then combine this mixture with the sponge, and add the caraway seeds. Work in the remainder of the rye flour. Turn the dough out onto a floured board and knead well. Place in a greased bowl, and brush the top with oil. Cover, and set in a warm place to rise until double in bulk. Shape into 2 long loaves. Brush with milk. Bake on greased cooky sheets at 325° F. for 1½ to 2 hours. Yields 2 long loaves.

SOUR-DOUGH RYE BREAD

SOUR DOUGH:

½ tablespoon dry yeast granules
1 cup warm water
1 cup rye flour

Soften the yeast in the water. When it bubbles, stir in the rye flour. Cover the mixture, and allow it to rise and fall again, without stirring or punching down. Keep the mixture at room temperature 2 to 3 days, or until it smells sour and has a sticky consistency. It is now ready to use, or to refrigerate for later use.

BREAD:

Since sour-dough bread rises slowly, begin making it in the morning.

2 cups sour dough
6 cups warm water
20 cups rye flour
½ cup blackstrap molasses
½ cup brewer's yeast
2 tablespoons sea salt or kelp
1 cup nonfat dry skim milk

Mix the sour dough with the water and 6 cups of the rye flour. Cover the mixture, and allow to stand in a warm place for at least 3 hours. The longer it stands, the sourer the taste of the bread. For sour dough for the next baking session, scoop out 2 cups of the mixture, place in a clean crock, cover, and refrigerate. Mix the rest of the mixture with the rest of the flour. Then blend in the remaining ingredients. Knead the dough until it is smooth and elastic. Shape into 4 loaves, and place on greased cooky sheets. Cover, and set in a warm place to rise for 3 to 4 hours. The loaves will only rise about ⅓ more than the former size. Bake at 350° F. for 1¼ to 1½ hours. Yields 4 round loaves.

COARSE SOUR-DOUGH RYE BREAD

10 cups rye flour
lukewarm water
2 tablespoons lemon juice or yogurt
1 tablespoon sea salt or kelp
¼ cup unsulfured molasses
1 tablespoon caraway seeds

Place 5 cups of the rye flour in a large bowl or bucket. Mix with enough water to moisten. Add the lemon juice or yogurt, to hasten the souring process. Cover the mixture, and allow it to stand in a warm place for 3 days, or until it begins to ferment. Add the remaining flour, the salt (or kelp), molasses, and caraway seeds. Then add enough additional warm water to make a pliable dough, one that can be worked and kneaded in the bowl or bucket. Knead 10 to 15 minutes, or until the dough holds together. Turn the dough onto a floured board, and shape into 4 loaves. Place on greased cooky sheets. Bake at 350° F. for 15 minutes, and then at 275° F. for about 2 hours. Yields 3 round loaves.

When first baked, the crust is very hard, and the inside is moist. The bread should be wrapped and stored for 2 days before serving.

FIVE-GRAIN PUMPERNICKEL

1 tablespoon dry yeast granules
2 cups warm water
⅓ cup unsulfured molasses
⅓ cup honey
1 teaspoon sea salt or kelp
2 cups rye flour
1 cup undegerminated yellow cornmeal
1 cup soy flour
½ cup peanut flour
6 cups wholewheat flour (about)

Soften the yeast in the warm water. When it bubbles, add the molasses, honey, salt (or kelp), rye flour, cornmeal, soy flour, and peanut flour. Then add enough wholewheat flour to make a stiff dough. Turn the dough out onto a floured board, and knead. Form into a ball, and place in a greased bowl. Oil the top, and cover. Set in a warm place to rise for 6 to 7 hours. Shape into 3 balls, and place on greased cooky sheets. Allow to rise slightly, and bake at 375° F. for about 1¼ hours. Yields 3 round loaves.

SEVEN-GRAIN PUMPERNICKEL

1 tablespoon dry yeast granules
1½ cups warm water
1 tablespoon honey
2 teaspoons sea salt or kelp
1 cup oat flour
½ cup rice flour
½ cup barley flour
½ cup undegerminated yellow cornmeal
½ cup rye flour
½ cup soy grits
4 cups wholewheat flour (about)

Soften the yeast in the warm water, with the honey added. When this mixture bubbles, add the salt (or kelp), oat, rice, and barley flours, cornmeal, rye flour, and soy grits. Then add enough wholewheat flour to make a stiff dough. Shape the dough into a ball, and place it in a greased bowl. Brush the top with oil. Cover, and set in a warm place to rise for 2 hours. This is a heavy dough and will not double in bulk. Shape it into 2 loaves, and place them on greased cooky sheets. Set in a warm place for 10 minutes. Then bake at 325° F. for about 1¼ hours. Yields 2 round loaves.

POTATO PUMPERNICKEL

3 cups water
¼ cup unsulfured molasses
1 cup potatoes, cooked and mashed
1 tablespoon sea salt or kelp
2 tablespoons dry yeast granules
7 cups rye flour
½ cup undegerminated yellow cornmeal
2 cups wholewheat flour (about)
additional cornmeal

Mix in a saucepan 2½ cups of water with the molasses, potatoes, and salt (or kelp). Bring to a boil, and then cool to lukewarm. Soften the yeast in ½ cup of warm water. When the yeast mixture bubbles, add the cooled potato mixture. Then add the rye flour, cornmeal, and 1 cup of the wholewheat flour. Mix by hand. Then let the dough rest 10 minutes. Knead about 10 minutes, working in enough of the remaining wholewheat flour to make the dough lose most of its stickiness. Place the dough in a greased bowl, and oil the top. Cover, and set in a warm place to rise for 1½ hours. Turn the dough out onto a floured board, and knead for 3 or 4 minutes. Let the dough rest on the board, covered, until it rises somewhat, about half-doubled. Knead lightly, and shape into 3 balls. Grease cooky sheets, and strew some cornmeal on them. Place the 3 balls on top of the cornmeal. Allow them to rise for 20 minutes in a warm place. Brush the loaves with water. Bake at 375° F. for about 1¼ hours. Yields 3 round loaves.

LENTIL PUMPERNICKEL

2 tablespoons dry yeast granules
4 cups water
¼ cup honey
1 cup lentils, soaked and drained
1 tablespoon sea salt or kelp
¼ cup oil
1 cup rye flour
1 cup gluten flour
1 cup millet flour
1 cup barley flour
4 cups wholewheat flour (about)

Soften the yeast in 1 cup of the water, with the honey added. Place the remaining 3 cups of water in an electric blender. Add the lentils, salt (or kelp), and oil. Blend until smooth. Add the lentil mixture to the bubbling yeast mixture. Stir thoroughly. Then add the rye, gluten, millet, and barley flours. Finally, add enough wholewheat flour to make a moderately stiff dough. Turn the dough out onto a floured board, and knead until smooth and elastic. Shape into 4 balls, and place on greased cooky sheets. Using a sharp knife, make crisscross slashes across the top of the balls. Cover with a moist cloth, and allow to rise somewhat. Bake at 350° F. for 50 to 60 minutes. Yields 4 round loaves.

LIMA BEAN FLOUR BREAD

1 tablespoon dry yeast granules
1¾ cups warm milk
1 tablespoon honey
1 tablespoon oil
¼ cup nonfat dry-milk powder
¼ cup wheat germ
⅓ cup soy flour
2 teaspoons sea salt or kelp
1 cup lima bean flour*
4¼ cups unbleached white flour (about)

Soften the yeast in the milk, with the honey added. When the yeast mixture bubbles, add the oil, milk powder, wheat germ, soy flour, salt (or kelp), and lima bean flour. Then add enough white flour to make a moderately stiff dough. Turn the dough out onto a floured board, and knead until it is smooth and elastic. Roll into a ball, place in a greased bowl, and oil the top. Cover, and set in a warm place to rise until double in bulk. Punch down, turn out onto a floured board, and knead lightly. Shape into 2 loaves, and place in greased bread pans. Cover, and set in a warm place for 2 to 3 hours to rise somewhat. Bake at 400° F. for 15 minutes, and then at 350° F. for 30 to 40 minutes longer. Yields 2 loaves.

* To make lima bean flour, grind dry lima beans in an electric blender or electric seed mill, ¼ cupful at a time.

LIMA BEAN FLOUR–RAISIN BREAD

1 tablespoon dry yeast granules
2 cups warm water
¼ cup honey
2 tablespoons oil
2 teaspoons sea salt or kelp
¼ cup raisins
1 cup lima bean flour*
1 cup oat flour
1½ cups wholewheat flour (about)

Soften the yeast in the water, with the honey added. When this mixture bubbles, add the oil, salt (or kelp), raisins, lima bean flour, and oat flour. Then add enough wholewheat flour to make a light, soft dough. Place in a bowl, cover, and set in a warm place to rise for 3 hours. Beat the dough well, and turn into 2 greased, floured bread pans. Allow it to rise for another hour. Bake at 375° F. for 15 minutes, and then at 325° F. for 30 to 35 minutes longer. Yields 2 loaves.

* To make lima bean flour, grind dry lima beans in an electric blender or electric seed mill, ¼ cupful at a time.

Breads

CRUSTY AND SOFT, SWEETENED AND HERBED

CORNELL MIX BREAD

Cornell Mix Bread, developed at Cornell University by Dr. Clive M. McCay and associates, is also known as the Triple Rich Cornell Formula or High Protein Bread. The Cornell Mix Bread formula is as follows: for each cup of flour, first place in the measuring cup 1 tablespoon of soy flour, 1 tablespoon of nonfat dry milk powder, and 1 teaspoon of wheat germ. Then fill the remainder of the cup with unbleached flour. This formula attempts to restore many of the nutrients lost or destroyed in the milling of flour, and to raise the nutritional value of the bread loaf. The formula has been readily available to the baking industry, which by and large continues to ignore it. The appearance of bread made with the Cornell Mix is similar to that of commercial white bread; its flavor and nutrition are vastly superior. I have made slight adaptations from the original recipe.

2 tablespoons dry yeast granules
3 cups warm water
2 tablespoons honey
6 cups sifted Cornell Mix (about)
1 tablespoon sea salt or kelp
2 tablespoons oil

Soften the yeast in the water, with the honey added. When this mixture bubbles, add to it 3 cups of the Cornell Mix and the salt (or kelp). Beat the mixture vigorously, using about 75 strokes by hand, or 2 minutes with an electric mixer. Add the oil, and enough of the remaining Cornell Mix to make a moderately stiff dough. Turn the dough out onto a floured board, and knead until it is smooth and elastic. Shape the dough into a ball, place in a greased bowl, and oil the top. Cover, and set in a warm place to rise until double in bulk (about 45 minutes). Punch the dough down, fold over the edges, and turn it upside down in the bowl, to rise another 20 minutes. Again, turn the dough out onto the floured board. Divide the dough into 3 parts. Fold each one inward to make a smooth, tight ball. Cover the balls with a cloth, and let them rest 10 minutes. Shape the balls into 3 loaves, and place in greased bread pans. Let the loaves of dough rise in the pans until they double in bulk (about 45 minutes). Bake at 325° F. for 45 to 50 minutes. Yields 3 loaves.

CRUSTY BREAD

3 tablespoons dry yeast granules
3 cups warm water
⅓ cup honey
3 tablespoons oil
1 cup nonfat dry milk powder
1 tablespoon sea salt or kelp
6½ cups wholewheat flour (about)
melted butter

Soften the yeast in the water, with the honey added. When the yeast mixture bubbles, add the oil, milk powder, and salt (or kelp). Then add enough wholewheat flour to make a moderately stiff dough. Turn the dough out onto a floured board, and knead until smooth and elastic. Shape into 2 long loaves, and place on greased cooky sheets. Place in a warm oven (80° to 85° F.), and allow to rise for 15 minutes. Remove the loaves of dough from the oven, and raise the oven temperature to 350° F. Return the loaves to the oven, and bake for 50 to 55 minutes. Brush the tops with melted butter. Yields 2 long loaves.

CRUSTY FRENCH BREAD

1 tablespoon dry yeast granules
2 cups warm water
2 tablespoons honey
2 tablespoons oil
2 teaspoons sea salt or kelp
4½ cups wholewheat flour (about)
cornmeal
¼ cup sesame seeds
1 tablespoon butter, melted

Soften the yeast in the warm water, with the honey added. When the yeast mixture bubbles, add the oil and salt (or kelp). Then add enough wholewheat flour to make a thick batter. Beat well with a spoon. Place in a bowl, cover, and set in a warm place to rise. For 5 consecutive times, work through the dough with a spoon at 10-minute intervals. Then turn the dough out onto a floured board, and divide it in half. Shape into 2 balls. Cover the balls of dough with a damp cloth, and allow to rest for 10 minutes. Then roll each ball into a 12x9-inch rectangle. Roll each rectangle firmly, as with a jelly roll. Seal the edges. Place the loaves on greased cooky sheets which have been sprinkled with cornmeal. Make 6 diagonal slashes across the top of each loaf with a sharp knife. Brush the tops lightly with cold water. Allow the loaves to rise until almost double in bulk. Brush again with cold water, and sprinkle with sesame seeds. Bake at 375° F. for 35 to 40 minutes. Brush with melted butter while still warm. Yields 2 long loaves.

CRUSTY ITALIAN BREAD

1 tablespoon dry yeast granules
2 cups warm water
1 tablespoon honey
1 teaspoon sea salt
¼ cup nonfat dry milk powder
¼ cup soy flour
¼ cup wheat germ
5½ cups unbleached white flour (about)

Soften the yeast in the warm water, with the honey added. When this mixture bubbles, add the salt, milk powder, soy flour, and wheat germ. Then add enough unbleached white flour to make a soft dough. Turn the dough out onto a lightly floured board, and knead until smooth and elastic. Shape the dough into a ball, place it in a greased bowl, and brush the top with oil. Cover, and set in a warm place to rise until double in bulk. Punch the dough down, and knead it lightly once again on the floured board. Divide the dough into 2 balls, and let them stand for 10 minutes. Roll the balls into 2 long slender loaves, and place them on greased cooky sheets. Cover loosely with a towel, and set in a warm place to rise until double in bulk. Before placing the loaves in the oven, put a flat pan filled with hot water in the bottom of the oven. This will insure the crustiness of the bread. Bake the bread at 425° F. for 10 minutes, and then reduce the heat to 350° F. and bake 10 minutes longer, or until golden brown. Yields 2 long loaves.

BRAIDED EGG BREAD

This is an adapted version of the traditional challah.

1 tablespoon dry yeast granules
½ cup warm water
2 tablespoons honey
1 tablespoon sea salt
¼ cup oil
4 cups warm water
4 eggs, beaten
¼ cup soy flour
¼ cup wheat germ
1 cup nonfat dry milk powder
16 cups unbleached white flour (about)
1 egg yolk, beaten
¼ cup poppy seeds

Soften yeast in water, with honey. When the mixture bubbles, add the next 8 ingredients, using enough unbleached white flour to make a stiff dough. Turn the dough out onto a lightly floured board, and knead until smooth and elastic. Place in a greased bowl, and brush the top with oil. Cover, and set in a warm place to rise until double in bulk. Turn half the dough onto the floured board, and cut into 4 equal parts. Roll each part into a long roll. Fasten the 4 rolls well at one end, and twist into a 4-ply braid (1 over 2, 3 over 4, 4 over 1, 2 over 4, 1 over 3, 3 over 2, etc.). To hold the braid, fasten the other end well. Braid the other half of the dough. Place the two breads on greased cooky sheets, brush with beaten egg yolk, and sprinkle with poppy seeds. Let rise until light. Bake at 400° F. for 15 minutes, and at 350° F. for 40 to 45 minutes longer. Yields 2 breads.

EGG–SESAME BREAD

2 tablespoons dry yeast granules
1 cup warm water
2 cups milk, scalded and cooled to warm
1 tablespoon sea salt or kelp
5 tablespoons vegetable oil
¼ cup honey
3 raw eggs, beaten
9 cups wholewheat flour (about)
½ cup sesame seeds

Soften the yeast in ½ cup of warm water. Mix together the milk, the rest of the water, the sea salt (or kelp), the oil and honey. When the yeast bubbles, combine the two mixtures and add the beaten eggs. Blend in seven cups of the wholewheat flour, and mix thoroughly. Allow the dough to rest for 10 minutes. Then add enough wholewheat flour to knead the dough easily. Turn out onto a lightly floured board and knead until smooth and elastic. Place in greased bowl and oil the top. Cover, and allow to rise in a warm place until double in bulk. Punch down, turn out onto a floured board and knead again. Cover, and return to warm place to rise again. Punch down, shape into three loaves, and place in greased bread pans. Brush the tops with oil, and sprinkle with sesame seeds. Allow to rise for the third time. Bake at 400° F. for 15 minutes, then at 375° F. for 30 minutes more. Yields 3 loaves.

PROTEIN BREAD

1½ cups soy flour
1½ cups wheat germ
¾ cup whey powder
2 tablespoons honey
3 cups milk
6 egg yolks, beaten
6 egg whites, beaten stiffly

Blend together thoroughly the soy flour, wheat germ, whey powder, honey, milk, and egg yolks. Fold in the egg whites. Turn the batter into a greased 15x9x2-inch pan. Bake at 300° F. for 50 to 60 minutes. Loosen the edges with a knife, and cut the bread into 1½ x 1½-inch squares. Yields 60 squares.

ENRICHED BREAD

1 tablespoon dry yeast granules
¼ cup warm water
2 tablespoons honey
1 tablespoon oil
2 teaspoons sea salt or kelp
1 tablespoon bone meal
1 tablespoon soy flour
1 tablespoon nonfat dry milk powder
1 tablespoon potato flour
2 tablespoons wheat germ
5⅓ cups oat flour (about)

Soften thc yeast in the warm water, with the honey added. When the yeast mixture bubbles, add the oil and salt (or kelp). Then add the bone meal, soy flour, milk powder, potato flour, and wheat germ. Finally, add enough oat flour to make a moderately stiff dough. Turn the dough out onto a lightly floured board, and knead for 8 minutes, or until smooth and elastic. Place the dough in a lightly greased bowl, turning it once to grease the surface. Cover, and set in a warm place to rise until double in bulk (1 to 1½ hours). Punch down, and let rise again until double in bulk (about 45 minutes). Divide the dough in half, and shape each half into a smooth ball. Cover, and let rest for 10 minutes. Shape into loaves, and place in 2 greased bread pans. Let rise until double in bulk (about 1 hour). Bake at 400° F. for 30 to 35 minutes. If, after the first 15 minutes in the oven, the tops are browning too rapidly, lower the heat to 350° F. Yields 2 loaves.

POTATO BREAD

1 tablespoon dry yeast granules
$\frac{1}{2}$ cup warm potato water
$\frac{1}{3}$ cup honey
$\frac{1}{2}$ cup oil
3 eggs
1 cup milk
1 cup potatoes, cooked and mashed
1 teaspoon sea salt or kelp
8 cups oat flour (about)
melted butter

Soften the yeast in the potato water. When this mixture bubbles, add the honey, oil, eggs, milk, potatoes, and salt (or kelp). Then add enough oat flour to make a stiff dough. Place the dough in a greased bowl, and brush the top with oil. Cover, and set in a warm place until doubled in bulk. Turn the dough out onto a lightly floured board, and knead well. Shape into 2 loaves, and place the loaves in greased bread pans. Cover, and let rise again until the dough is light. Bake at 375° F. for 45 to 50 minutes. Brush the baked loaves with melted butter. Yields 2 loaves.

SOY-CAROB BREAD

1 tablespoon dry yeast granules
3 cups warm water
1 cup honey
½ cup oil
½ cup nonfat dry milk powder
½ cup sunflower seed meal
1 cup soy flour
1 cup carob powder
6 cups wholewheat flour (about)

Soften the yeast in the water, with the honey added. When this mixture bubbles, add to it the oil, milk powder, sunflower seed meal, soy flour, and carob powder. Then add enough wholewheat flour to make a stiff dough. Turn the dough out onto a floured board, and knead until smooth and elastic. Shape the dough into a ball, place in a greased bowl, oil the top, and cover. Set the dough in a warm place to rise until double in bulk. Then punch it down, knead lightly, and let rise once again. Shape the dough into 2 loaves, and place them in greased bread pans. Let rise again. Bake at 375° F. for 45 to 55 minutes. Yields 2 loaves.

SUNFLOWER SEED BREAD

2 tablespoons dry yeast granules
1 cup warm water
3 tablespoons honey
2 teaspoons sea salt or kelp
2 cups sunflower seed meal
4 cups wholewheat flour (about)
melted butter

Soften the yeast in the water, with the honey added. When this mixture bubbles, add the salt (or kelp) and sunflower seed meal. Then add enough wholewheat flour to make a moderately stiff dough. Turn the dough out onto a floured board, and knead until smooth and elastic. Divide the dough into 2 balls, shape into loaves, and place in greased bread pans. Set the oven for 150° F. and place the loaves in it for 15 minutes. Remove the loaves, and raise the oven temperature to 350° F. Then return the loaves to the oven, and bake 35 to 40 minutes longer. Brush the tops with melted butter. Yields 2 loaves.

NUT BREAD

1 tablespoon dry yeast granules
2 cups warm water
¼ cup honey
½ cup nonfat dry milk powder
1 teaspoon sea salt or kelp
1⅔ cups nutmeats, ground
2 cups wholewheat flour
2 cups oat flour (about)

Soften the yeast in the water, with the honey added. When the yeast mixture bubbles, add the milk powder, salt (or kelp), nutmeats, and wholewheat flour. Then add enough oat flour to make a stiff dough. Turn the dough into 2 greased bread pans, and allow to rise until double in bulk. Bake at 375° F. for 50 to 60 minutes. Yields 2 loaves.

SWEET POTATO BREAD

1 tablespoon dry yeast granules
¼ cup warm water
⅓ cup honey
3 tablespoons oil
1 cup milk
1 cup sweet potatoes, cooked and mashed
1 teaspoon sea salt or kelp
5 cups oat flour (about)

Soften the yeast in the water. When the mixture bubbles, add the honey, oil, milk, potatoes, and salt (or kelp). Then add enough oat flour to make a soft dough. Place the dough in a greased bowl, and brush the top with oil. Cover, and set in a warm place to rise until double in bulk. Shape into 3 loaves, and place in greased bread pans. Let rise again until the dough is light. Bake at 350° F. for 20 to 25 minutes. Yields 3 loaves.

ONION BREAD

1 tablespoon dry yeast granules
1 cup warm water
⅓ cup honey
¼ cup oil
1 teaspoon sea salt or kelp
3 tablespoons nonfat dry milk powder
3 tablespoons soy flour
3 tablespoons wheat germ
⅔ cup gluten flour
2 cups wholewheat flour
2⅓ cups unbleached white flour (about)
1 cup onions, chopped and sautéed

Soften the yeast in the warm water, with the honey added. When the yeast mixture bubbles, add the oil, salt (or kelp), milk powder, soy flour, wheat germ, gluten flour, and wholewheat flour. Then add enough unbleached white flour to make a moderately stiff dough. Turn the dough out onto a lightly floured board, and knead until smooth and elastic. Shape into a ball, place in a greased bowl, and brush the top with oil. Cover, and set in a warm place to rise until double in bulk. Turn the dough out again onto the floured board, and knead lightly. Return the dough to the bowl, add the onions, and work them into the dough uniformly. Shape the dough into 2 round balls, and place them on greased cooky sheets. Bake at 375° F. for 15 minutes, and then at 325° F. for 15 to 20 minutes longer. Yields 2 round loaves.

TANGY CHEESE BREAD

1 tablespoon dry yeast granules
¾ cup warm water
2 tablespoons honey
2 tablespoons butter
2 eggs
1 cup milk
1 teaspoon sea salt or kelp
½ teaspoon sweet paprika, ground
1¼ cups sharp Cheddar cheese, grated
4¾ cups wholewheat flour (about)
1 egg yolk, beaten
⅓ cup sesame seeds

Soften the yeast in the water, with the honey added. When the mixture bubbles, add the butter, eggs, milk, salt (or kelp), paprika, and cheese. Then add enough wholewheat flour to make a stiff dough. Turn the dough out onto a lightly floured board, and knead until smooth and elastic. Shape into a ball, place in a greased bowl, and brush the top with oil. Cover, and set in a warm place to rise until double in bulk. Turn the dough out onto the floured board again, and knead lightly for 1 minute. Divide the dough in half, and shape into loaves. Place in greased bread pans. Brush the tops with the beaten egg yolk, and then sprinkle them with the sesame seeds. Cover, and let rise in a warm place for about 40 minutes. Bake at 350° F. for 15 minutes, and then reduce the heat to 325° F. for 25 to 30 minutes longer. Yields 2 loaves.

COTTAGE CHEESE BREAD

1 tablespoon dry yeast granules
½ cup warm water
¼ cup honey
2 tablespoons oil
2 cups cottage cheese, well drained
1 raw onion, grated
1 tablespoon dill seeds, ground
2 teaspoons sea salt or kelp
2 eggs, beaten
5 cups wholewheat flour (about)
melted butter

Soften the yeast in the water. When the yeast mixture bubbles, add the honey, oil, cottage cheese, onion, dill seeds, salt (or kelp), and eggs. Then add enough wholewheat flour to make a thick batter. Beat the batter well. Cover, and set in a warm place to rise until double in bulk (about 1 hour). Stir down the batter, and turn it into 2 greased 1-quart casseroles. Cover, and set in a warm place to rise until light. Bake at 350° F. for 40 to 50 minutes, or until golden brown. Brush with melted butter. Yields 2 round loaves.

HERBED BREAD

2 tablespoons dry yeast granules
$\frac{1}{4}$ cup warm water
2 tablespoons honey
$\frac{1}{4}$ cup oil
2 teaspoons sea salt or kelp
2 cups milk
1 teaspoon fresh or green-dried marjoram, minced
2 teaspoons fresh or green-dried thyme, minced
$7\frac{1}{2}$ cups wholewheat flour (about)
melted butter

Soften the yeast in the water, with the honey added. When the mixture bubbles, add the oil, salt (or kelp), milk, marjoram, and thyme. Then add enough wholewheat flour to make a stiff dough. Turn the dough out onto a lightly floured board, and knead until smooth and elastic. Shape it into a ball, place in a greased bowl, and brush the top with oil. Cover, and set in a warm place to rise, for about 1 hour. Return the dough to the floured board. Punch it down, knead it lightly, and shape it into 2 loaves. Place the loaves in greased bread pans, cover with a damp cloth, and set in a warm place to rise until almost double in bulk. Brush the tops with melted butter. Bake at 375° F. for 30 to 35 minutes. Yields 2 loaves.

HERBED SEEDED BREAD

4 cups warm water
½ cup oil
1 tablespoon poppy seeds
1 tablespoon caraway seeds
1 tablespoon dill seeds
1 tablespoon celery seeds
¼ cup raw onion, grated
¼ cup fresh parsley, minced
1 teaspoon oregano, minced
1 tablespoon sea salt or kelp
2 tablespoons dry yeast granules
¼ cup honey
4 eggs, beaten
9 cups wholewheat flour (about)
melted butter

Blend in a saucepan 3½ cups of the water with the oil, 4 kinds of seeds, onion, parsley, oregano, and salt (or kelp). Bring to the boiling point, remove from the heat, and cool to lukewarm. Soften the yeast in the remaining ½ cup warm water, with the honey added. When the yeast mixture bubbles, combine it with the lukewarm herb-seed mixture. Then add enough wholewheat flour to make a thick batter. Beat it vigorously for 2 minutes. Cover, and set in a warm place to rise until double in bulk. Stir down with a spoon, and beat hard for 1 minute. Turn into 2 greased round 2-quart casseroles. Let rise for 10 minutes. Bake at 350° F. for 40 to 45 minutes. Brush with melted butter. Yields 2 round loaves.

HERB-FILLED BREAD

DOUGH:

1 tablespoon dry yeast granules
$1\frac{3}{4}$ cups warm water
$2\frac{1}{2}$ tablespoons honey
$\frac{1}{4}$ cup oil
$1\frac{1}{4}$ cups milk
2 teaspoons sea salt or kelp
$7\frac{1}{2}$ cups wholewheat flour (about)

FILLING:

2 eggs, beaten
2 cloves garlic, minced
1 cup fresh dill, minced
2 cups fresh parsley, minced
1 cup of the green parts of scallions, minced
2 tablespoons butter, melted

Soften the yeast in $\frac{1}{4}$ cup of the water, with the honey added. When the mixture bubbles, add the oil, milk, and salt (or kelp). Add 2 cups of the wholewheat flour, and beat vigorously for 2 minutes. Cover, and set in a warm place to bubble up and form a sponge (about 1 hour). Add the remaining $1\frac{1}{2}$ cups of warm water. Then add enough of the remaining $5\frac{1}{2}$ cups of wholewheat flour to form a moderately stiff dough. Turn the dough out onto a floured board, and knead until smooth and elastic. Shape into a ball, place in a greased bowl, brush the top with oil, and cover. Set in a warm place to rise for about 30 minutes.

Again, turn the dough out onto a floured board, and knead. Divide the dough in half and shape into 2 balls. Cover the balls with a damp cloth, and allow them to rest for 10 minutes. Then roll each ball, with a rolling pin, into a rectangle about 9 inches wide, and ¼ inch thick. Brush with a little of the beaten eggs to be used in the filling. Mix the remainder of the beaten eggs with the garlic, dill, parsley, and scallions. Spread this filling on the rolled dough, keeping it about 1 inch from the edges. Roll up the rectangles like jelly rolls, and pinch the edges to seal in the filling. Place these loaves, with seam sides down, in 2 greased bread pans. Brush the tops with melted butter. Cover, and set in a warm place to rise (about 1 hour). Bake at 350° F. for 20 minutes, and then at 325° F. for 20 to 25 minutes longer. Yields 2 loaves.

HERBED TOMATO JUICE BREAD

2 tablespoons dry yeast granules
$\frac{1}{2}$ cup warm water
$\frac{1}{4}$ cup honey
$\frac{1}{4}$ cup oil
$1\frac{1}{2}$ cups warm tomato juice
2 teaspoons sea salt or kelp
1 teaspoon oregano
2 tablespoons dill seeds
$5\frac{3}{4}$ cups wholewheat flour (about)
melted butter

Soften the yeast granules in the water. When the mixture bubbles, add the honey, oil, tomato juice, salt (or kelp), oregano, and dill seeds. Add enough wholewheat flour to make a stiff dough. Turn the dough onto a floured board, and knead until smooth and elastic. Shape into a ball, place in a greased bowl, oil the top, and cover. Set in a warm place to rise until double in bulk. Again, turn the dough out onto a floured board, and knead lightly. Divide the dough in half, and shape into balls. Place them on greased cooky sheets, and brush the tops with melted butter. Cover, and let rise in a warm place until doubled in bulk. Bake at 350° F. for 45 to 50 minutes. Yields 2 round loaves.

PEANUT BUTTER BREAD

2 tablespoons dry yeast granules
2 cups warm water
⅓ cup honey
7 cups wholewheat flour (about)
½ cup nonfat dry milk powder
⅔ cup peanut butter
2 eggs, beaten
1 tablespoon sea salt or kelp

Soften the yeast in the water, with the honey added. When this mixture bubbles, add 2 cups of the wholewheat flour. Blend, cover the bowl, and set in a warm place to allow the sponge to rise and be light. Blend together the milk powder, peanut butter, eggs, and salt (or kelp). Add this mixture to the sponge. Stir in enough of the remaining wholewheat flour so that the dough follows the spoon around the bowl. Turn the dough out onto a floured board, and knead until smooth and elastic. Shape into a ball, and place in a greased bowl. Oil the surface of the dough, and cover it. Set the bowl in a warm place to allow the dough to rise and double in bulk. Punch down, and allow the dough to rise again. Shape into 2 loaves and place them in greased bread pans. Allow the loaves to rise until double in bulk. Bake at 375° F. for 25 to 30 minutes. Yields 2 loaves.

Rolls

Because many recipes for bread dough may also be used for rolls, you can save time by doubling a bread recipe and shaping half of it into rolls. They need not be shaped and baked on the same day as the bread baking. If you prefer, refrigerate the dough intended for rolls, and complete them on another day.

Bake rolls at a higher temperature than breads, but reduce the total baking time. The smaller the rolls, the quicker they will bake. If you wish, you can add an egg to the roll dough for extra color, flavor, and nourishment. For each egg you add, reduce the oil by 1 tablespoonful.

Rolls freeze well, and they thaw out quickly. To restore their freshness, reheat them briefly in an oven set at a low heat.

Rolls can be shaped in various ways. It is fun to try them:

Bowknots: Roll the dough under your palms to ½-inch thickness. Cut these into pieces about 6 inches long and ½ inch wide. Tie each piece into a single knot.

Twists: Roll the dough and cut it the same as for bowknots. Hold one end of the strip of dough in each hand, and twist the ends in opposite directions. Bring the two ends together, forming a shape like a rope.

Braids: Roll the dough and cut it the same as for bowknots. Press the top ends of three strips together, braid the strips, and press the bottom ends together. If you want to be extra fancy, make a four-ply braid (1 over 2, 3 over 4, 4 over 1, 2 over 4, 1 over 3, 3 over 2, etc.)

Cloverleafs: Shape small pieces of dough into balls, about the size of a walnut, by rolling them between your palms. Place 3 balls in each well of greased muffin pans.

Leaf buds: Shape pieces of dough into balls, slightly larger than for cloverleafs. Place only 2 in each muffin well.

Crescents: Roll a ball of dough into a round ¼-inch thick. Cut the round into pie-shaped wedges. Brush with melted butter. Roll up, beginning at the wide end. Press the tip of the wedge gently so that the rolled roll does not open. Curve each roll into a semicircle, or a crescent. Or, roll the dough out into a square sheet of ⅛-inch thickness. Cut the sheet into 6-inch squares, cut each square in half, from corner to corner, to form triangles. Then, roll up in the same way as the wedge.

Fan tans: Roll a piece of dough into a very thin rectangular sheet. Brush it with melted butter, and cut into strips about 1 inch wide. Pile 6 strips one on top of another. Cut into 1½-inch-long pieces, and place on end, in the wells of greased muffin pans.

Pinwheels or Snails: Roll, cut, and brush the dough as for Fan tans, but cut the strips ½ inch wide. Roll each strip, like a jelly roll. Pinch the end firmly so that it will remain closed. Arrange on greased cooky sheets, with the cut side flat on the cooky sheet.

Pocketbooks or Parker House: Cut flattened dough with a round cooky cutter. Using the dull edge of a knife blade, crease through the center of each circle. Fold the dough over, and press the edges together.

What other shapes can you create?

WHOLEWHEAT CLOVERLEAF ROLLS

1 tablespoon dry yeast granules
2 cups warm water
¼ cup honey
¼ cup oil
1 tablespoon sea salt or kelp
¼ cup nonfat dry milk powder
6 cups wholewheat flour (about)
melted butter

Soften the yeast in the water, with the honey added. When this mixture bubbles, add the oil, salt (or kelp), and milk powder. Then add enough wholewheat flour to make a firm dough. Shape the dough into a ball, turn onto a floured board, and knead until smooth and elastic. Place in a greased bowl, brush the top with oil, cover, and set in a warm place to rise until double in bulk. Turn the dough out again onto the floured board, and knead lightly. Shape it into small balls, about ½ inch in diameter. Place 2 or 3 balls in each well of greased muffin pans. Brush with melted butter. Cover, and set in a warm place to rise until double in bulk. Bake at 400° F. for 15 to 20 minutes. Yields about 2½ dozen medium-sized rolls.

WHOLEWHEAT POCKETBOOK ROLLS

1 tablespoon dry yeast granules
3 cups warm water
½ cup honey
¼ cup oil
2 eggs, beaten
2 teaspoons sea salt or kelp
7 cups wholewheat flour (about)
melted butter

Soften the yeast in the water, with the honey added. When the mixture bubbles, add the oil, eggs, and salt (or kelp). Then add enough wholewheat flour to make a soft dough. Turn the dough out onto a floured board, and let it rest for 10 minutes. Then knead it until it is smooth and elastic. Shape into a ball, place in a greased bowl, oil the top, and cover. Set in a warm place to rise until double in bulk (about 2 hours). Punch the dough down, and roll it to about ½-inch thickness. Cut out 3-inch rounds. Make a deep crease down the center of each round, and flatten one half slightly. Brush with melted butter, and fold the thicker half over the thinner one. Place on greased cooky sheets, 1 inch apart. Set in a warm place, to rise until double in bulk. Bake at 400° F. for 15 to 20 minutes. Yields about 3 dozen rolls.

GLUTEN-SOY ROLLS

1 tablespoon dry yeast granules
2 cups warm water
2 teaspoons unsulfured molasses
2 tablespoons oil
2 eggs, beaten
1 teaspoon sea salt or kelp
½ cup nonfat dry milk powder
1 cup gluten flour
1 cup soy flour
3 cups unbleached white flour (about)

Soften the yeast in the water, with the molasses added. When the mixture bubbles, add the oil, eggs, salt (or kelp), milk powder, and gluten and soy flours. Then add 1 cup of the unbleached white flour. Beat until well blended, and bubbly. Add enough of the remaining unbleached white flour to make a stiff dough. Turn the dough out onto a floured board, and knead until smooth and elastic. Place in a greased bowl, oil the top, and cover. Set in a warm place to rise until double in bulk. Punch down, and knead lightly. Allow the dough to rise again. Punch down again, and shape into rolls. Place the rolls on greased cooky sheets, allowing space between. Bake at 375° F. for 20 to 25 minutes. Yields 5 to 6 dozen rolls.

WHEAT GERM ROLLS

1 tablespoon dry yeast granules
1 cup warm water
1 tablespoon honey
1 egg, beaten
1 teaspoon sea salt or kelp
¾ cup wheat germ
⅓ cup nonfat dry milk powder
2½ cups wholewheat flour (about)
melted butter

Soften the yeast in the water, with the honey added. When this mixture bubbles, add the egg, salt (or kelp), wheat germ, and milk powder. Then add enough flour to make a soft dough. Beat the dough for 2 minutes. Cover, and set in a warm place to rise until double in bulk (about 1 hour). Shape into rolls, and place on greased cooky sheets, allowing space between. Brush the tops lightly with melted butter. Cover the rolls, and allow them to rise until double in bulk. Bake at 350° F. for 20 to 25 minutes, or until golden brown. Yields 20 2-inch rolls.

RYE ROLLS

1 tablespoon dry yeast granules
¼ cup warm water
⅓ cup honey
¼ cup oil
2 eggs, beaten
½ teaspoon sea salt or kelp
1 cup milk
½ cup corn flour
3 cups rye flour (about)

Soften the yeast in the water. When the yeast mixture bubbles, add the honey, oil, eggs, salt (or kelp), milk, and corn flour. Then add enough rye flour to make a soft dough. Refrigerate overnight. Turn the dough out onto a floured board, and knead lightly. Shape into rolls. Place on greased cooky sheets. Set in a warm place to rise until double in bulk (about 4 hours). Bake at 450° F. for 25 to 30 minutes. Yields 2 dozen rolls.

RYE–CARAWAY SEED ROLLS

1 tablespoon dry yeast granules
1¼ cups warm water
1 tablespoon unsulfured molasses
1 teaspoon sea salt or kelp
3 tablespoons nonfat dry milk powder
2 tablespoons soy flour
2 tablespoons wheat germ
2¼ cups rye flour
1¾ cups unbleached white flour (about)
2 tablespoons caraway seeds

Soften the yeast in the water, with the molasses added. When this yeast mixture bubbles, add the salt (or kelp), milk powder, soy flour, wheat germ, and rye flour. Then add enough unbleached white flour to make a soft dough. Turn the dough out onto a floured board, and knead until smooth and elastic. Place in a greased bowl, oil the top, and cover. Set in a warm place, to rise until double in bulk (about 2 hours). Punch the dough down, and allow it to rise again (about 1½ hours). Turn the dough out onto the floured board again, and knead lightly. Cover, and allow to rest for 10 minutes. Shape into rolls, and place on greased cooky sheets, allowing space between. Using a sharp knife, make a gash lengthwise on top of each roll. Brush the tops with cold water, and sprinkle with the caraway seeds. Place a pan of boiling water on the top shelf of the oven, set at 400° F. Bake the rolls on the lower shelf, for 20 to 25 minutes. Yields 3 dozen rolls.

CORN FLOUR ROLLS

1 tablespoon dry yeast granules
2½ cups warm water
3 tablespoons honey
2 eggs, beaten
4 cups corn flour (about)
¼ cup soy flour
2 tablespoons oil
1 teaspoon sea salt or kelp

Soften the yeast in the water, with the honey added. When the mixture bubbles, add the eggs and 1 cup of the corn flour. Beat well, and set in a warm place for ½ hour. Then add the soy flour, oil, and salt (or kelp), with enough corn flour to make a soft but firm dough. Stir the mixture well. Cover, and set in a warm place to rise until double in bulk. Punch down, shape into rolls, place on greased cooky sheets, and allow to rise 2 hours. Bake at 400° F. for 12 to 15 minutes. Yields 4 dozen rolls.

CORNMEAL ROLLS

- **⅓ cup honey**
- **⅓ cup oil**
- **2 cups milk**
- **1 cup undegerminated yellow cornmeal**
- **1 teaspoon sea salt or kelp**
- **1 tablespoon dry yeast granules**
- **½ cup warm water**
- **2 eggs, beaten**
- **5 cups wholewheat flour (about)**

Combine, in the top of a double boiler, the honey, oil, milk, cornmeal, and salt (or kelp). Cook over hot water, stirring constantly, until the mixture reaches a boil. Remove from the heat, and cool to lukewarm. Soften the yeast in the water. When the yeast mixture bubbles, add it to the lukewarm cornmeal mixture. Add the eggs. Then add enough wholewheat flour to make a soft dough. Turn the dough out onto a floured board, and knead until smooth and elastic. Shape into a ball, place in a greased bowl, oil the top, and cover. Set in a warm place, to rise until double in bulk. Punch the dough down, turn it out again onto the floured board, knead lightly, and shape into rolls. Place the rolls on greased cooky sheets, allowing space between, and set them in a warm place to rise until double in bulk. Bake at 400° F. for 5 minutes, and then at 375° F. for about 10 to 12 minutes longer. Yields 4 dozen rolls.

POTATO ROLLS

1 cup potatoes, raw and diced
2 cups water
3 cups unbleached white flour
1 cup oat flour
3 tablespoons soy flour
3 tablespoons wheat germ
3 tablespoons nonfat dry milk powder
1½ teaspoons sea salt or kelp
2 teaspoons dry yeast granules
1 tablespoon honey
3 tablespoons oil

Cook the potatoes in the water until soft. Drain, and save 1 cup of the potato water, or if necessary, add more water to make 1 cup of liquid. Mash the potatoes. Mix together the white, oat, and soy flours, the wheat germ, milk powder, and salt (or kelp). Soften the yeast in 1 cup of warm potato water. When the yeast mixture bubbles, combine it with the dry ingredient mixture. Add the potatoes, honey, and oil. Blend thoroughly, and turn out onto a floured board. Knead the dough until smooth and elastic. Shape into a ball, place in a greased bowl, oil the top, and cover. Set in a warm place, to rise until double in bulk. Without kneading the dough again, pinch off small pieces, shape them into small balls the size of a walnut, and place three balls in each greased well of muffin pans. Set the pans in a warm place, to rise until double in bulk. Bake at 375° F. for 20 to 25 minutes, or until golden brown. Yields 4 dozen rolls.

THREE-GRAIN ROLLS

1 tablespoon dry yeast granules
¼ cup warm water
¼ cup honey
1 cup milk
¼ cup oil
1 teaspoon sea salt or kelp
2 eggs, beaten
1 cup undegerminated yellow cornmeal
½ cup oat flour
2⅔ cups wholewheat flour (about)

Soften the yeast in the water. When the mixture bubbles, add the honey, milk, oil, salt (or kelp), eggs, cornmeal, and oat flour. Then add enough wholewheat flour to form a stiff dough. Turn the dough out onto a floured board, and knead until smooth and elastic. Shape into a ball, place in a greased bowl, oil the top, and cover. Set in a warm place, to rise until double in bulk. Punch down, and shape into rolls. Place the rolls on greased cooky sheets. Set in a warm place, to rise until double in bulk. Bake at 375° F. for 25 to 30 minutes. Yields 4 dozen rolls.

QUICKIE YEAST ROLLS

3 tablespoons dry yeast granules
⅓ cup warm water
1 tablespoon honey
¼ cup butter, softened
1 cup milk, scalded, cooled to lukewarm
3 tablespoons wheat germ
3 tablespoons soy flour
¾ teaspoon sea salt or kelp
4 cups unbleached white flour
1¾ cups oat flour (about)

Soften the yeast in the water, with the honey added. When this mixture bubbles, add the butter, milk, wheat germ, soy flour, salt (or kelp), and unbleached white flour. Then add enough oat flour to form a stiff dough. Turn the dough out onto a floured board, and knead until smooth and elastic. Shape into a ball, place in a greased bowl, oil the top, cover, and place in an oven set at 85° F. Leave the dough in the oven for 15 minutes. Then punch down the dough, knead it lightly, and shape it into rolls. Place the rolls on greased cooky sheets, allowing space between. Return to the 85° F. oven, and allow to rise until double in bulk. Remove from the oven, and set the temperature at 400° F. Bake at this temperature for 15 to 20 minutes. Yields about 3½ dozen rolls.

NO-KNEAD ROLLS

½ cup oil
1 tablespoon sea salt or kelp
¼ cup honey
2 cups boiling water
2 tablespoons dry yeast granules
½ cup warm water
2 eggs
⅓ cup wheat germ
½ cup nonfat dry milk powder
⅓ cup soy flour
3 cups unbleached white flour
3½ cups oat flour (about)
melted butter

Measure into a large bowl the oil, salt (or kelp), honey, and boiling water. Mix thoroughly, and cool to lukewarm. Soften the yeast in warm water. When the yeast mixture has bubbled, combine with the lukewarm mixture. Add the eggs. Gradually mix in half of the wheat germ, milk powder, soy, white, and oat flours, or enough so that the batter can be beaten easily without splashing. Beat the batter until smooth. Continue to add the dry ingredients until the dough no longer clings to the bowl. If it is not necessary, do not use the full amount of oat flour. Turn the dough into a large greased bowl, cover, and chill in the refrigerator for 24 hours. Punch down the dough, and shape it into rolls. Place the rolls on greased cooky sheets, allowing space between. Brush with melted butter, and set in a warm place to rise until double in bulk. Bake at 400° F. for 20 to 25 minutes. Yields about 3 dozen rolls.

CRISP ROLLS

This is an adaptation of semmel, a traditional crusty roll.

1 tablespoon dry yeast granules
2 cups warm milk
1 tablespoon sea salt or kelp
½ cup wheat germ
3 tablespoons soy flour
2 cups oat flour
4½ cups unbleached white flour (about)
1 egg yolk, beaten with 1 teaspoon cold water

Soften the yeast in the milk. When the yeast mixture bubbles, add the salt (or kelp), wheat germ, soy flour, oat flour, and 1 cup of the unbleached white flour. Beat this mixture thoroughly, place in a bowl, cover, and set in a warm place to rise. When the sponge is light, add enough of the remaining unbleached white flour to make a moderately stiff dough. Turn the dough out onto a floured board, and knead until smooth and elastic. Turn the dough into a greased bowl, oil the top, and cover. Set in a warm place to rise. Punch the dough down. Pinch off pieces of it and shape into rolls 1 inch high and 3 inches across. Place the rolls on greased cooky sheets, allowing space between. Dip the handle of a knife into flour, and then press it down through the center of each roll, lengthwise, and roll it back and forth to make a deep crease through the middle of the roll. Put the rolls in a warm place to rise. Then brush with the egg yolk mixture. Bake at 400° F. for 15 to 20 minutes, or until crisp and brown. Yields 3½ to 4 dozen rolls.

MILK ROLLS

This is an adaptation of the recipe for traditional Austrian rolls.

7½ cups unbleached white flour
⅓ cup wheat germ
¼ cup soy flour
1 teaspoon sea salt or kelp
½ cup butter, softened
1 tablespoon dry yeast granules
2 cups of milk, scalded, cooled to warm
1 egg, beaten
additional milk, scalded, cooled to warm (if needed)

Blend together the unbleached white flour, wheat germ, soy flour, and salt (or kelp). Rub the butter into this dry mixture, and make a well in the center of it. Soften the yeast in the 2 cups of warm milk. When the mixture bubbles, pour it into the well in the center of the dry mixture. Mix well to form a soft dough. If the dough is too stiff, add more scalded, warm milk. Turn the dough out onto a floured board and knead until smooth and elastic. Put into a warm bowl, and cover with a cloth. Set in a warm place to rise until double in bulk (about 1 hour). Turn the dough out again onto a floured board, and knead again. Shape into rolls, place on warmed greased cooky sheets, and allow to rest for 10 to 20 minutes. Glaze the tops of the rolls with egg. Bake at 400° F. for 20 to 25 minutes, or until golden brown. Yields 8 large rolls, or 16 small rolls.

FEATHER-WEIGHT ROLLS

1 tablespoon dry yeast granules
¼ cup warm water
¼ cup honey
½ cup butter, melted
1¾ cups scalded milk, cooled to lukewarm
2 eggs, beaten
¾ teaspoon sea salt or kelp
3 tablespoons nonfat dry milk powder
2 tablespoons wheat germ
1 tablespoon soy flour
2 cups unbleached white flour
2 cups oat flour (about)

Soften the yeast in the water. When it bubbles, add the honey, butter, milk, eggs, salt (or kelp), milk powder, wheat germ, soy flower, and white flour. Then add enough oat flour to make a batter only slightly stiffer than for cake. Beat thoroughly. Cover, and set in a warm place to rise. When light, pour into greased muffin tins until the tins are ⅔ full. Let rise until the tins are full (about 1 hour). Bake at 400° F. for 10 to 12 minutes. Yields 2 to 2½ dozen rolls.

SESAME SEED ROLLS

1 tablespoon dry yeast granules
1 cup warm water
⅓ cup honey
¼ cup oil
1 teaspoon sea salt or kelp
¼ cup nonfat dry milk powder
3 tablespoons wheat germ
3 tablespoons soy flour
1 cup unbleached white flour
1 cup oat flour
1 cup wholewheat flour (about)
1 egg yolk, beaten
½ cup sesame seeds

Soften the yeast in the water. When it bubbles, add to it the honey, oil, salt (or kelp), milk powder, wheat germ, and soy, white, and oat flours. Then add the wholewheat flour, using only enough to form a moderately stiff dough. Turn the dough out onto a floured board, and knead until smooth and elastic. Shape into a ball, place in a greased bowl, oil the top, and cover. Set in a warm place to rise until double in bulk. Punch the dough down, knead it lightly, and return it to the bowl. Cover, and allow to rise again. Shape the dough into balls 1½ inches in diameter. Place 1 ball in each well of well-greased muffin pans. Brush the tops of the balls with beaten egg yolk, and sprinkle with sesame seeds. Set in a warm place to rise. Bake at 425° F. for 15 to 20 minutes. Yields about 2 dozen rolls.

CARAWAY SEED CRESCENT ROLLS

1 tablespoon dry yeast granules
¼ cup warm water
¼ cup honey
⅓ cup oil
1 cup milk, scalded, and cooled to lukewarm
1½ teaspoons sea salt or kelp
¼ cup wheat germ
⅓ cup soy flour
3 cups unbleached white flour
3 cups oat flour (about)
2 tablespoons butter, melted
¼ cup caraway seeds

Soften the yeast in the water. Measure into a large bowl the honey, oil, milk, and salt (or kelp). Mix thoroughly. When the yeast mixture has bubbled, combine the 2 mixtures. Gradually add the wheat germ and flours, using only enough oat flour to make a stiff dough. Turn the dough out onto a floured board, and knead until smooth and elastic. Place in a greased bowl, oil the top, cover, and set in a warm place to rise until double in bulk. Punch down, knead, and divide into 4 equal parts. Roll each part into a ball, and allow to rest for 10 minutes. Roll out each ball into a circle ¼ inch thick. Cut each circle into 8 wedge-shaped pieces. Roll up each piece, starting with the wide end. Bend into a semicircle. Place on greased cooky sheets, allowing space between. Brush with butter, and sprinkle with caraway seeds. Cover, and set in a warm place to rise until double in bulk. Bake at 425° F. for 10 minutes. Yields 2⅔ dozen crescent rolls.

POPPY SEED ROLLS

This is an adaptation of a recipe for traditional Biálys.

2 tablespoons dry yeast granules
2 cups warm water
¼ cup honey
⅓ cup oil
2 teaspoons sea salt or kelp
½ cup nonfat dry milk powder
2 tablespoons wheat germ
2 tablespoons soy flour
⅓ cup gluten flour
1¼ cups unbleached white flour
3 cups wholewheat flour (about)
1 cup poppy seeds

Soften the yeast in the water, with the honey added. When the mixture bubbles, add all other ingredients except the poppy seeds. Use only enough wholewheat flour, to make a stiff dough. Turn out onto a floured board, and knead until smooth and elastic. Shape into a ball, place in a greased bowl, oil the top, and cover. Set in a warm place to rise. When the dough is light, punch it down, and shape it into 24 balls. Cover these, and let rise until light. Pull balls into long rolls. Place the rolls on greased cooky sheets. Make a deep thumbprint in the center of each roll, pour into it about a teaspoonful of poppy seeds, and pinch the dough closed around the seeds. Brush the tops of the rolls with cold water, and sprinkle with additional poppy seeds. Set in a warm place to rise again. Bake at 375° F. for 15 to 20 minutes. Yields 2 dozen poppy seed rolls.

CORIANDER SEED ROLLS

2 tablespoons dry yeast granules
2 cups warm water
$\frac{1}{4}$ cup honey
$\frac{1}{3}$ cup oil
2 teaspoons sea salt or kelp
$\frac{1}{3}$ cup gluten flour
$1\frac{1}{4}$ cups oat flour
3 cups wholewheat flour (about)
2 tablespoons coriander seeds, ground

Soften the yeast in the water, with the honey added. When this mixture bubbles, add to it the oil, salt (or kelp), gluten flour, and oat flour. Then add the wholewheat flour, using only enough to make a stiff dough. Turn the dough out onto a floured board, and knead until smooth and elastic. Shape into a ball, place in a greased bowl, oil the top, and cover. Set in a warm place to rise. When the dough is light, punch it down, and pinch off pieces of it to make rolls 6 inches long and $\frac{1}{2}$ inch wide. Place 3 rolls together, pinch them together firmly at one end, braid them, and pinch them together firmly at the other end. Place on greased cooky sheets. Brush with water, and sprinkle with coriander seeds. Cover, and allow to rise. Bake at 375° F. for 15 to 20 minutes. Yields 2 dozen coriander seed rolls.

ALMOND CRESCENTS

1 tablespoon dry yeast granules
$\frac{1}{4}$ cup warm water
$\frac{1}{4}$ cup honey
1 cup milk, scalded and cooled to warm
$\frac{1}{4}$ cup oil
1 teaspoon sea salt or kelp
3 eggs, beaten
6 cups wholewheat flour (about)
$\frac{1}{2}$ cup slivered almonds

Soften the yeast in the water with the honey. When the mixture bubbles, add the milk, oil, sea salt or kelp, and eggs. Beat well. Then add enough flour to make the dough a good consistency. Knead until smooth and elastic. Place in greased bowl, oil the top, cover, and set in a warm place to rise until double in bulk. Punch down. Allow to rise again, and punch down. Divide dough in two parts. Shape into 2 balls and roll each ball into a twelve-inch circle. Cut each circle into eight pie-shaped wedges. Roll each wedge from the broad end, forming crescents. Place on greased cooky sheets and brush with oil. Sprinkle almonds on top, and set in a warm place to rise until double in bulk. Bake at 400° F. for 15 to 20 minutes. Makes 16 crescents.

ONION ROLLS

1 tablespoon dry yeast granules
1 cup warm water
⅓ cup honey
¼ cup oil
1 teaspoon sea salt or kelp
¼ cup nonfat dry milk powder
3 tablespoons soy flour
3 tablespoons wheat germ
1 teaspoon bone meal
⅓ cup gluten flour
1⅔ cups unbleached white flour
1 cup wholewheat flour (about)
1 cup onions, chopped and sautéed

Soften the yeast in the water, with the honey added. When the mixture bubbles, add to it the oil, salt (or kelp), milk powder, soy flour, wheat germ, bone meal, gluten flour, and unbleached white flour. Add the wholewheat flour, using only enough to form a moderately stiff dough. Turn the dough out onto a floured board, and knead until smooth and elastic. Shape into a ball, place in a greased bowl, oil the top, cover, and set in a warm place to rise until double in bulk. Punch the dough down, work in the onions, and shape into rolls. Place on greased cooky sheets, allowing space between. Cover with a damp cloth, and set in a warm place to rise until double in bulk. Bake at 425° F. for 15 to 20 minutes. Yields about 2 dozen rolls.

BAGELS

This is an adaptation of a recipe for a popular, traditional Jewish roll, dubbed at times "a varnished doughnut" or "a petrified doughnut."

1 tablespoon dry yeast granules
⅔ cup warm water
2 tablespoons honey
1 egg, beaten
3 tablespoons oil
1 teaspoon sea salt or kelp
3 tablespoons nonfat dry milk powder
2 tablespoons soy flour
2 tablespoons wheat germ
3 cups unbleached white flour (about)

Soften the yeast in the water, with the honey added. When the mixture bubbles, add the remaining ingredients, using only enough unbleached white flour to make a stiff dough. Turn the dough out onto a floured board, and knead until smooth and elastic. Shape the dough into a ball, put in a greased bowl, oil the top, and cover. Set in a warm place to rise for 45 minutes. Turn the dough out onto a floured board, and knead again. Divide the dough into 12 pieces. Flour your hands, and roll the pieces into 8-inch strips. Form the strips into circles, pressing the two ends together securely. Place the bagels on a floured cooky sheet, and broil for 4 minutes. Remove, and drop into boiling water. Cover, and simmer for 20 minutes. Drain well. Place, once again, on the floured cooky sheet. Bake at 400° F. for 15 minutes, or until browned on both sides. Yields 1 dozen bagels.

Little Breads

HAMBURGER BUNS

2 tablespoons dry yeast granules
¼ cup warm water
3 tablespoons honey
3 tablespoons oil
1 egg, beaten
1 teaspoon sea salt or kelp
3½ cups wholewheat flour (about)
¼ cup sesame seeds

Soften the yeast in the water. When the mixture bubbles, add the honey, oil, egg, and salt (or kelp). Blend thoroughly, and allow to rise for 10 minutes. Then add enough wholewheat flour to make a soft dough. Turn the dough out onto a floured board, and knead until it is smooth and elastic. Shape into round, flat buns, and place on greased cooky sheets, allowing space between. Brush the tops of the buns with cold water, and sprinkle with sesame seeds. Cover the buns, and set in a warm place, to rise until double in bulk. Bake at 375° F. for 15 minutes. Yields 2 dozen buns.

RAISED POTATO BISCUITS

1 tablespoon dry yeast granules
¼ cup warm water
⅓ cup honey
¾ cup oil
1 cup milk
2 eggs, beaten
1½ teaspoons sea salt or kelp
5½ cups wholewheat flour (about)
1 cup cooked mashed potatoes

Soften the yeast in the water. When the mixture bubbles, add to it the honey, oil, milk, eggs, potatoes, and salt (or kelp). Then add 1 cup of the wholewheat flour, and beat well. Cover, and set in a warm place to rise. Then add enough of the remaining wholewheat flour to make a soft dough. Cover the dough, and set it in a warm place to rise. Turn the dough onto a floured board, pat, and roll to ¼-inch thickness. Shape with a small round cutter, and place biscuits on greased cooky sheets, with space between. Set in a warm place and allow the dough to rise. Bake at 425° F. for 12 to 15 minutes. Yields about 3 dozen small biscuits.

Note: After the dough is made, with the second addition of flour, it can be refrigerated for several days, and the biscuits baked only as needed. If the dough has been refrigerated, allow more rising time before baking.

SUNFLOWER SEED BISCUITS

1 tablespoon dry yeast granules
⅔ cup warm water
1 tablespoon honey
6 tablespoons oil
1½ teaspoons sea salt or kelp
3 tablespoons nonfat dry milk powder
1 cup sunflower seed meal
1 cup wholewheat flour (about)

Soften the yeast in the water, with the honey added. When the mixture bubbles, add the remainder of ingredients, using only enough wholewheat flour to make a soft, but firm dough. Shape into biscuits, and place on greased cooky sheets. Allow to rise. Bake at 375° F. for 10 to 12 minutes. Yields about 1½ dozen small biscuits.

RAISED BISCUITS

This is an adaptation of a recipe for Southern-style biscuits.

1 tablespoon dry yeast granules
¼ cup warm water
1 tablespoon sorghum syrup
2 cups milk
2 tablespoons oil
6 cups wholewheat flour (about)
1 egg, beaten
melted butter

Soften the yeast in the water, with the sorghum added. When this mixture bubbles, add the milk, oil, and 2 cups of wholewheat flour. Beat well, and cover. Set the batter in a warm place, to rise until double in bulk. Stir it down. Add the egg, and enough of the remaining wholewheat flour to make a soft dough. Turn the dough out onto a floured board, and knead until smooth and elastic. Roll out the dough to ½-inch thickness. Cut with a biscuit cutter. Dip the biscuits in a bit of melted butter, and place on cooky sheets about 1 inch apart. Allow to rise until double in bulk. Bake at 400° F. for 20 to 25 minutes. Yields 4 dozen biscuits.

BRIOCHES

This is an adaptation of a traditional French roll.

1 tablespoon dry yeast granules
¾ cup warm water
4¾ cups unbleached white flour (about)
4 eggs
½ cup butter, melted
⅓ cup oil
1 tablespoon honey
1¼ teaspoons sea salt
3 tablespoons nonfat dry milk powder
2 tablespoons soy flour
2 tablespoons wheat germ
2 tablespoons milk

Soften the yeast in the water. When this bubbles, stir in 1 cup of unbleached white flour. Cover, and set in a warm place to rise. When the mixture is light, add to it the eggs, butter, oil, honey, salt, milk powder, soy flour, and wheat germ. Then add enough of the remaining unbleached white flour to make a soft dough. Beat. Cover, and allow to rise until double in bulk. Beat again. Grease the surface of the dough, and refrigerate overnight. Pinch off pieces of dough the size of a plum, and place in greased muffin pans. Set in a warm place to rise. When light, brush with milk. Bake at 400° F. for 20 to 25 minutes, or until golden brown. Yields 2½ to 3 dozen brioches.

CROISSANTS

This is an adaptation of a traditional French roll.

1 tablespoon dry yeast granules
½ cup warm milk
1 egg yolk, beaten in 1 tablespoon of lukewarm water
1 tablespoon oil
½ teaspoon honey
½ teaspoon sea salt
2 tablespoons wheat germ
2 tablespoons soy flour
2 cups unbleached white flour
⅔ cup sweet butter, softened
additional egg yolk, beaten with 1 teaspoon cold milk

Soften the yeast in the warm milk. When the mixture bubbles, add to it the egg yolk, oil, honey, salt, wheat germ, soy flour, and white flour. Blend thoroughly, and turn out onto a floured board. Knead the dough until smooth and elastic. Shape into a ball, and place in a *dry* mixing bowl. Cover, and set in a warm place to rise until double in bulk (about 2 hours). Turn the dough out onto the floured board again, and knead lightly. Roll the dough out to ⅛-inch thickness, keeping it as square in shape as possible. Place the butter, in one lump, in the center of the square. Fold over it each corner of the dough square, as if making an envelope. Roll out the dough again in the same way, and fold it again in the same way. For the third time, roll it out, and fold it. Then chill the dough for 15 minutes. Repeat this rolling and chilling 4 times. Then form the dough into a ball, place it in a cold earthenware bowl, and cover it with a cloth soaked in ice-cold water and well wrung-out. Chill the dough for 30 minutes, or longer. Again, roll the dough out into a square of ⅛-inch thickness. Cut the dough into 6-inch squares. Cut each square in half, from corner to corner, to form triangles. Starting with the wide end of the triangle, roll each loosely, ending with the point, and curve to make a crescent. Place the croissants on lightly floured cooky sheets, and set them in a warm place until they have doubled in bulk (about 1 hour). Brush them with the egg yolk beaten with cold milk. Bake at 400° F. for 5 minutes, and then at 350° F. for 15 or 20 minutes longer, or until golden brown. Yields 2 dozen croissants.

WHOLEWHEAT ENGLISH MUFFINS

1 tablespoon dry yeast granules
½ cup warm water
1 cup scalded milk, cooled to lukewarm
2 tablespoons oil
4 cups wholewheat flour (about)
1½ teaspoons sea salt or kelp

Soften the yeast in the water. When this bubbles, add the milk, oil, and 2 cups of the wholewheat flour. Mix well, and cover. Set this sponge in a warm place to rise, for about an hour. Mix together the salt (or kelp) and the remaining 2 cups of wholewheat flour. When the sponge is light, add to it enough of the salted wholewheat flour to make a soft dough. Beat the dough well. Cover, and set in a warm place to rise. When the dough is double in bulk, turn it out onto a floured board, and lightly work in a little flour. Roll the dough out into a sheet of about 1-inch thickness. Cut into large rounds, cover, and allow to rise for about an hour. Bake slowly on both sides, on a lightly greased griddle. Yields about 1½ dozen muffins.

Serve these muffins hot. To do so, split and butter the cold muffins, and toast them.

Crackers, Hardtack, Flat Breads, Patties

Because many recipes for bread dough may also be used for crackers as well as for rolls, you can save time by doubling a bread recipe, and using part of the dough for crackers. If the bread dough is too soft to roll thin for crackers, chill it first. This will make it easier to roll. Or, add more flour.

Because of the thinness of crackers, they should be baked briefly. Crackers freeze well, and thaw out quickly. They are good for snacks, as a garnish for soups and salads, for lunch boxes and picnic baskets.

Crackers can be shaped in various ways. They can be scored into squares or diamonds. They can be rolled out, and cut with cooky cutters. Before being baked, they can be pricked with the tines of a fork to prevent blown up "pillows."

WHOLEWHEAT CRACKERS

4 cups wholewheat flour
1 teaspoon celery seeds, ground
1 teaspoon caraway seeds, ground
1 teaspoon dill seeds, ground
½ cup oil
1 cup boiling water (about)

Mix together the flour and the ground seeds. Add the oil, and mix until crumbly. Add enough boiling water to make the mixture of a good consistency to hold together. Turn out onto a floured board, and roll out thin. Cut into squares, and place on greased cooky sheets. Bake at 375° F. for 25 to 30 minutes. Yields about 4 dozen crackers.

HERBED WHOLEWHEAT CRACKERS

1½ cups milk
1 cup butter, softened
1 tablespoon sea salt or kelp
1 cup sesame seeds
1 teaspoon rosemary, crushed
5 cups wholewheat flour (about)

Blend all the ingredients together, using only enough wholewheat flour to make a firm dough that can be rolled. Turn the dough out onto a floured board, and roll very thin. Cut into cracker shapes, and place on greased cooky sheets. Bake at 375° F. for 10 to 15 minutes. Yields about 4 dozen crackers.

WHOLEWHEAT-GLUTEN CRACKERS

2 cups wholewheat flour
½ cup wheat germ
⅓ cup gluten flour
1 teaspoon sea salt or kelp
⅓ cup oil
1 cup cold water (about)

Combine all the ingredients, using only enough water to make a stiff dough. Knead for 5 minutes. Then roll out to ¼-inch thickness. Shape into crackers, and arrange on greased cooky sheets. Bake at 250° F. for 40 to 45 minutes. Yields about 2 dozen crackers.

RAISED WHOLEWHEAT-GLUTEN CRACKERS

1 tablespoon dry yeast granules
2 cups warm water
3 tablespoons honey
⅓ cup oil
1 teaspoon sea salt or kelp
⅓ cup gluten flour
1 cup oat flour
3½ cups wholewheat flour (about)

Soften the yeast in the water, with the honey added. When this mixture bubbles, add the remainder of the ingredients, using only enough wholewheat flour to make a firm dough. Turn the dough out onto a floured board, and knead. Place in a greased bowl, oil the top, and cover. Set in a warm place, to allow the dough to rise somewhat. Roll out to ¼-inch thickness. Cut into cracker shapes, and place on greased cooky sheets. Allow to rise slightly, and then prick each cracker with the tines of a fork. Bake at 375° F. for 20 to 25 minutes. Yields 4 dozen crackers.

WHOLEWHEAT–SUNFLOWER SEED MEAL CRACKERS

½ cup oil
¼ cup honey
3 cups wholewheat flour
1 cup sunflower seed meal
¼ cup wheat germ
1 teaspoon sea salt or kelp
1 cup cold water (about)

Combine all the ingredients, in the order given, adding only enough water to make a stiff dough. Knead the dough. Roll it out to ¼-inch thickness. Cut into cracker shapes, and place on greased cooky sheets. Bake at 350° F. for 8 to 10 minutes, or until golden brown. Yields 5 dozen crackers.

SESAME SEED CRACKERS

1 cup sesame seeds
1 teaspoon sea salt or kelp
2 cups wholewheat flour
⅔ cup butter
¼ cup ice water (about)

Blend together the sesame seeds, salt (or kelp), and wholewheat flour. Cut in the butter. Then add enough ice water to make the dough the consistency of piecrust. Roll out very thin. Cut into small rounds. Place on greased cooky sheets. Bake at 325° F. for 15 to 20 minutes. Yields about 3 dozen small crackers.

OAT-NUT CRACKERS

2 cups water
3 tablespoons honey
1 cup nutmeats, ground
¼ cup sesame seeds, ground
4 cups oat flour (about)

Blend all the ingredients together, adding only enough oat flour to make the dough a good consistency to hold together. Turn the dough out onto a floured board, and knead. Roll out to ¼-inch thickness. Cut into cracker shapes. Place on greased cooky sheets. Prick with the tines of a fork. Bake at 325° F. for 10 to 15 minutes. Yields about 3½ dozen crackers.

CHEESE CRACKERS

3 eggs
1 cup Cheddar cheese, diced
1 cup oil
1 cup undegerminated yellow cornmeal
½ cup brown rice flour
½ cup wheat germ
¼ cup sesame seeds
½ cup milk

Blend the eggs and the Cheddar cheese in an electric blender. Turn the mixture into a bowl, and add the remaining ingredients. Blend thoroughly. The batter will be loose. Drop by the teaspoonful onto greased cooky sheets, allowing space between for the crackers to spread. Bake at 375° F. for 10 to 12 minutes. Cool on paper toweling to absorb the excess oil from the cheese. Yields 4 dozen crackers.

SOY-CHEESE CRACKERS

1¼ cups soy flour
1 teaspoon sea salt or kelp
3 egg yolks, beaten
¼ cup milk
1 cup sharp Cheddar cheese, grated

Blend together the flour and the sea salt (or kelp). Add the egg yolks and milk slowly, and blend thoroughly. Add the cheese, and mix well. Turn the dough out onto a floured board, and roll it thin. Cut into 2-inch squares. Place on greased cooky sheets. Bake at 350° F. for 8 to 10 minutes, or until browned. Yields about 3 dozen crackers.

HARDTACK

This is an adaptation of a recipe for a traditional Swedish cracker.

1 tablespoon dry yeast granules
¼ cup warm water
½ cup honey
3 cups buttermilk
½ cup oil
2 teaspoons sea salt or kelp
1 cup oat flour
1 cup wheat germ
3 cups rye flour (about)

Soften the yeast in the water. When this bubbles, add the remaining ingredients, using only enough rye flour to make a stiff dough. If the dough is sticky, add more rye flour. Roll the dough out very thin, and cut into any shapes desired. Place on greased cooky sheets. Set in a warm place, and allow to rise slightly. Prick each cracker with the tines of a fork. Bake at 350° F. for 8 to 10 minutes, or until lightly browned. When cool, store in a tightly closed container or freeze. Reheat to make crisp. Yields about 4 dozen crackers.

SWEDISH FLAT BREAD

1 tablespoon dry yeast granules
2¼ cups warm water
¼ cup unsulfured molasses
2 tablespoons oil
2 teaspoons sea salt or kelp
1 teaspoon caraway seeds, ground
1 teaspoon anise seeds, ground
3 tablespoons nonfat dry milk powder
3 tablespoons wheat germ
3 tablespoons soy flour
¼ cup gluten flour
2½ cups unbleached white flour
2½ cups rye meal (about)

Soften the yeast in the water, with the molasses added. When this mixture bubbles, add to it the remaining ingredients, using only enough rye meal to make a stiff dough. Turn the dough out onto a floured board, and knead. Place in a greased bowl, oil the top, and cover. Set in a warm place to rise somewhat. Knead again, and shape into circles of about ½-inch thickness. Place on greased cooky sheets. Prick each circle of dough with the tines of a fork. Allow to rise slightly. Bake at 400° F. for 20 to 25 minutes. Yields about 2½ dozen flat breads.

DANISH FLAT BREAD

1 tablespoon dry yeast granules
1 cup warm water
¼ cup honey
½ cup oil
1 teaspoon sea salt or kelp
1 cup graham flour
1 cup rye flour
4 cups oat flour (about)

Soften the yeast granules in the water. When this mixture bubbles, add the rest of the ingredients, using only enough oat flour to form a dough that will hold together. Turn the dough out onto a floured board, and roll it out into very thin circles. Allow the circles to rest for 10 minutes. Then bake each on a greased griddle, or on ungreased soapstone on the top of the stove over moderate heat, for only a few moments. Then transfer the circles to greased cooky sheets, and bake at 400° F. for 5 to 8 minutes, or until crisp and brown. Yields about 2½ dozen flat breads.

MIXED-GRAIN FLAT BREAD

This is an adaptation of a recipe for a traditional Scandinavian cracker.

½ cup rye flour
½ cup wheat flour
½ cup millet flour
½ cup oat flour
½ cup barley flour
½ cup rice flour
½ cup wheat germ
½ cup soy flour
½ cup nonfat dry milk powder
2 teaspoons sea salt or kelp
½ cup oil
3 tablespoons caraway seeds, ground
1½ cups cold water (about)

Blend all the ingredients together, using only enough water to make the dough a good consistency to hold together. Spread the dough out thinly and evenly on greased shallow pans. Bake at 200° F. for 50 to 60 minutes. Cut immediately into squares. Yields about 4 dozen crackers.

CORNMEAL-COCONUT PATTIES

2 cups undegerminated yellow cornmeal
1 cup dried coconut shreds, unsweetened
water

Blend the cornmeal and the coconut shreds together. Add to this blend enough water to moisten it and form a solid mass. Shape into balls, the size of a walnut, and place on lightly greased cooky sheets. Flatten each ball with the bottom of a glass dipped in cold water. Bake at 400° F. for 5 to 8 minutes, or until lightly browned. Yields about 2½ dozen patties.

Serve plain, or with cottage cheese, guacamole (mashed, seasoned avocado), or chicken salad.

Cookies

ROLLED, SHAPED, SPOONED, REFRIGERATED

"There is no such thing as a *good* cooky or confection," is a favorite statement of a dentist friend. He's right! All you have to do to *know* that he's right is to eat a cooky or confection, open your mouth, and examine it in front of a mirror. A lot of sticky debris is still clinging to the teeth.

Despite cookies being bad for your teeth, I am now presenting you with an entire section devoted to cookies and confections. The reason is that most people crave sweet desserts. They end their meals with sweets—such as cookies—or snack on them between meals. Physiologically, sweetness cuts off the appetite. For some, there is a sweet-dessert syndrome: a need to be countered with bitter coffee or tea; a need to be combined with cigarette, cigar, or pipe.

If you need to be weaned away from this craving for sweet desserts, and the rest of the syndrome, I propose that you do it sensibly. Serve fresh fruit, instead. However, it has been my observation that although most people like fruit, they don't consider it dessert, unless it comes in the form of apple pie, blueberry tart, or strawberry ice cream. When I serve fresh fruit to such people—no matter how attractive the fruit appears—these people look around as if something is missing.

As a result, I've learned to compromise. *Two* desserts are put on the table: fresh fruit *and* cookies. Some individuals eat the fruit as though they are being dutiful children who then demand their cooky reward. Others, wiser about food and nutrition, may eat *one* cooky, but make certain to finish the meal with the fruit. They use nature's own scrubbing action of apples, or other fruit, to cleanse the teeth. A few others—strong-willed characters—forego the cookies completely, and limit their desserts solely to fruit.

I purposely make cookies in small sizes, for this reduces the total intake of sweet desserts. But it does more than that. Do you remember when miniature chocolate candies were first sold? The confectionery industry had been told by motivational researchers that many people had a sense of guilt when they indulged in eating candy. The industry was informed that bite-size miniature chocolate candies would relieve this sense of guilt. Industry took the advice. Sales soared, and, correspondingly, guilt complexes fell. By the same token, people feel less shameful about reaching for a small cooky than for a large one.

Serve only one variety of cooky at a time. Human nature being what it is, people want to try whatever is presented. If there are several kinds of tempting cookies on a plate, people feel unfulfilled until they have tried some of each, thus upping the total consumed. Keep the total low by deliberately not presenting a variety of cookies at any one time.

Since cookies are going to be eaten, they should at least be made with wholesome ingredients. For many years I used wholewheat flour as the basic flour and honey or molasses as a sweetener. One day, a natural-foods friend commented to me, while munching away on a sample from the latest batch, "The trouble with nutritious cookies is *that they all taste the same.*" I knew exactly what she meant. No matter how many variations I attempted, using dried fruits, nuts, seeds, and other ingredients, that wholewheat flavor, or the honey and molasses flavors, seemed to predominate. Once you tasted one nutritious cooky, you had tasted them all.

This started me thinking. Is it really necessary to use the traditional wholewheat flour? Are there alternatives? Knowing that some individuals cannot tolerate wholewheat, or the coarse bran in the wheat, I sought help from other sources. I discovered that there are other nutritious flours, quite suitable for cooky making, which can substitute entirely, or in part, for wholewheat. These flours can result in delicious cookies, and they give the adventurous cook the possibility of exciting experimentation. For my own taste, oat flour is highly satisfactory. It is easy to handle, and it gives cookies an excellent flavor. At first, I merely ground up raw rolled oats in an electric blender, and used this meal as flour. However, I discovered that commercially available oat flour is finer in texture, and is therefore better for many recipes.

Then I began to experiment with natural sweeteners. I had always used a bland honey for certain types of cookies, and a combination of unsulfured molasses and blackstrap molasses for others. I found that many of the same ones suitable in bread baking were also good for cookies. (See Page 6). There are still other natural sweeteners to use. Cinnamon gives an illusion of sweetness to baked goods, even if it does not actually add sweetness. Date powder, which is nothing more than pulverized ground dates, looks very much like brown sugar. It even "cakes" hard, as brown sugar does. These are all ingredients that allow the cooky maker to omit or to cut down on other sweetening agents listed in recipes.

What else have I done to change cooky recipes? In an attempt to reduce the total salt intake in the diet, I decided that salt could safely be eliminated from cooky recipes without any disastrous results. When a cooky has flavor from sweeteners, from fruits or spices, why should salt be necessary? I've eliminated it from cooky recipes, and, to date, no one has complained.

I have also eliminated all recipes requiring baking powder, baking soda, or cream of tartar. Many, many old cooky recipes did not depend on leaveners other than eggs or oven heat. Cookies are generally chewy or crisp, rather than light and fluffy. So out went the vitamin-destroying leaveners.

As a busy person whose time is precious, I usually plan to

make batches of different kinds of cookies during one working period. I find this plan to be both a timesaver and a worksaver. Many of the same ingredients are required for different recipes. Once they are assembled, there they are. The same mixing bowls and baking sheets can be used again and again, without repeating the need for taking them out of their storage place, washing, drying, and putting them away again. The oven is going steadily. Time is not wasted.

Cookies can be rolled out and cut into fancy shapes, molded, dropped by the spoon, refrigerated and cut, or turned into pans and then cut into bars and squares. I find that the bars and squares are easiest. The dough can be patted into the pans, and quickly cut into shapes. It takes infinitely longer to roll out dough or shape it into balls. However, I have included all types of cookies in the recipes that follow.

In our household, cookies are *not* eaten daily. They are reserved for meals with guests, or for other special occasions such as birthdays and holidays. This means using the deep freeze to store cookies. They freeze well. I use empty two-quart plastic milk containers for freezing them. The cookies can be packed in these containers and removed from them without crumbling. The pointed-top milk containers, if opened completely, can be pressed down to form a flat surface that excludes air. Because of their rectangular shape, these containers stack readily in a freezer. They use space efficiently. With a thick marking pen, I write the names of the cookies on the sides of the containers. If guests drop in unexpectedly, frozen cookies are thawed out by the time the coffee has perked, the tea has brewed, or the hot carob has been prepared.

For many of the cooky recipes that follow, you will note that flour measures are "about." My experience has been that the amounts of flour needed vary, depending on many factors. For example, the type of flour used—western hard wheat or eastern soft wheat; the fineness or roughness of the grinding;

the freshness of the grinding; the size of the eggs. For this reason, you, the cooky maker, will have to bear in mind the one-word instruction my grandmother gave with recipes: *according.* Judge "according" to the way the dough looks and feels. If the dough is for drop cookies, it should be thin enough to spoon onto the sheets. If it is to be rolled into balls, it must bind together more firmly, "according."

By the same token, I find that oven baking varies from one stove to another. Baking temperatures and baking time may vary for your stove and mine. Once again, the watchword is "according." Time the first batch of cookies, and you will have a check for subsequent batches.

In testing a new recipe, whether it is one given by a friend, or one that I am devising, I place only two or three cookies on the first cooky sheet that is put in the oven. This gives me an idea of how the batter bakes, if it spreads excessively, if the oven temperature is correct, and if the timing is successful. This trial run also shows me whether the cookies should be removed from the cooky sheets immediately after baking or be allowed to cool on the sheets, whether squares should be scored while still hot or should cool first. And since the proof is in the eating, it gives me a chance to sample the product. I can adjust the remainder of the batter for texture, sweetness and flavor, and adjust the oven for temperature or timing, if necessary. It prevents waste, and results in better cookies.

You are now ready, and set. Go!

HONEY-WHOLEWHEAT COOKIES

¾ cup honey
½ cup oil
2 eggs
½ teaspoon vanilla extract
2 cups wholewheat flour (about)
1 cup walnuts, broken

Blend the honey and the oil. Add the eggs, one at a time, and beat well after each addition. Add the vanilla, and enough of the flour to make a dough that holds together. Blend in the walnut pieces. Shape the dough into a roll, wrap in waxed paper, and chill until firm. Slice to about ¼-inch thickness, and place the slices on greased, floured cooky sheets. Bake at 375° F. for 10 to 12 minutes. Yields 2½ dozen cookies.

WHEAT GERM–ORANGE COOKIES

1 cup honey
½ cup oil
1 egg
¼ cup orange juice
1 teaspoon vanilla extract
1 cup wheat germ
1¾ cups graham flour

Blend all the ingredients together thoroughly, and drop by the tablespoonful onto greased cooky sheets. Bake at 350° F. for 8 to 10 minutes, or until brown. Yields about 4 dozen cookies.

OATMEAL COOKIES

½ cup honey
½ cup date sugar, firmly packed
1 cup oil
4 eggs
½ cup milk
2 teaspoons cinnamon, ground
1 teaspoon nutmeg, grated
2 cups rolled oats, uncooked
2 cups oat flour (about)

Blend all the ingredients together, in the order given, adding only enough oat flour to make the batter a good consistency to drop by teaspoonfuls onto greased cooky sheets. Bake at 350° F. for 18 to 20 minutes. Yields 5 dozen cookies.

OATMEAL-SESAME COOKIES

1 cup honey
1 cup oil
2 eggs
½ cup sesame seeds
2 cups oat flour
1½ cups rolled oats, uncooked
½ teaspoon ginger, ground

Blend all the ingredients together thoroughly. Drop by teaspoonfuls onto greased cooky sheets. Bake at 350° F. for 10 to 12 minutes. Yields 6 dozen cookies.

RICE FLOUR COOKIES

These cookies are oily but crisp.

¼ cup honey
½ cup oil
1 egg
2 teaspoons lemon juice
¾ cup soy grits
1½ cups brown rice flour

Blend all the ingredients together thoroughly. The dough will be quite moist, but it will hold together. Break off pieces of dough the size of a walnut, and shape into flat cookies, 1½ inches in diameter. Place on greased cooky sheets. Press the tops of the cookies with the tines of a fork, pressing one way, and then another, to form a crosshatch pattern. Bake at 350° F. for 8 to 10 minutes, or until golden. Yields 3½ dozen cookies.

ALL-RICE FLOUR COOKIES

1 cup honey
⅔ cup oil
2 eggs, beaten
1 teaspoon vanilla extract
1 cup nutmeats, broken
1 cup raisins, steamed
2¼ cups rice flour (about)

Blend all the ingredients together, using only enough rice flour to make the dough a good consistency to drop by teaspoonfuls onto greased cooky sheets. Bake at 350° F. for 12 to 15 minutes. Yields 5 dozen cookies.

ALL-BARLEY FLOUR COOKIES

⅔ cup honey
½ cup oil
1 egg, beaten
1 teaspoon almond extract
3 tablespoons milk
1 cup nutmeats, broken
2 cups barley flour (about)

Blend all the ingredients together, using only enough barley flour to make the dough a good consistency to drop by teaspoonfuls onto greased cooky sheets. Bake at 350° F. for 10 to 15 minutes. Yields 4 dozen cookies.

SOY–WHEAT GERM COOKIES

1 cup unsulfured molasses
1 cup oil
2 eggs
2 cups soy flour
1 cup wheat germ

Blend all the ingredients together thoroughly. The batter will be quite thin. Drop it by the teaspoonful onto greased cooky sheets, allowing space for the batter to spread. Bake at 300° F. for 12 to 15 minutes, or until browned at the edges. Yields 8 dozen 2-inch cookies.

SOY GRITS–BROWN RICE FLOUR COOKIES

¾ cup honey
½ cup oil
2 eggs
2 teaspoons vanilla extract
2 teaspoons cinnamon, ground
½ cup soy grits
1½ cups brown rice flour

Blend all the ingredients together thoroughly. Drop by teaspoonfuls onto greased cooky sheets. Bake at 350° F. for 10 to 12 minutes. Yields 4 dozen cookies.

POTATO FLOUR COOKIES

- 1 cup honey
- 1 cup oil
- 2 cups potato flour
- 2 eggs
- 2 teaspoons lemon extract

Blend all the ingredients together thoroughly. The dough will be quite firm. Pinch off pieces the size of a walnut, and shape into rounds 1½ inches in diameter and ¼-inch in thickness. Place on greased cooky sheets. Using the tines of a fork, press gently into the tops one way, and then the other way, making crosshatch marks. Bake at 300° F. for 15 to 18 minutes, or until golden brown. The cookies will become crisp as they cool. Yields 6½ dozen cookies.

FRUIT-SEED COOKIES

½ cup dates, pitted
½ cup raisins
½ cup hot water
⅔ cup honey
1 cup oil
2 eggs
2½ cups rolled oats, uncooked
½ cup rye flour
½ cup oat flour
1 cup sesame seeds
1 teaspoon cardamom seeds, ground

Soak the dates and the raisins in the hot water for ½ hour. Combine this mixture with the honey, oil, and eggs in an electric blender. Blend until smooth. Pour the blended mixture into a bowl, and add the remaining ingredients. Mix thoroughly, and shape into small balls the size of a walnut. Place on greased cooky sheets. Press flat with a fork. Bake at 350° F. for 10 to 12 minutes. Yields 6 dozen cookies.

HONEYED FRUIT COOKIES

1 cup honey
1 cup oil
2 eggs
½ cup prunes, pitted and cut into small pieces
½ cup dried unsulfured apricots, cut into small pieces
½ cup figs, cut into small pieces
1 teaspoon sea salt or kelp
1 teaspoon lemon extract
3 cups rolled oats, uncooked
1 cup wholewheat flour (about)

Beat together the honey, oil, and eggs. Add the remaining ingredients, using only enough wholewheat flour to make the dough a good consistency to drop by teaspoonfuls onto greased cooky sheets. Bake at 375° F. for 10 minutes. Let the cookies remain on the cooky sheets 2 minutes before removing. Yields 5 dozen cookies.

UNCOOKED FIG COOKIES

3 cups unsulfured dried figs
1 cup sunflower seeds
1 tablespoon brewer's yeast
2 teaspoons bone meal
water
¼ cup nutmeats, ground

Combine the figs and the sunflower seeds, and put through a meat grinder. Add the yeast, bone meal, and enough water to make the dough a good consistency to hold together. Shape into small balls the size of a walnut. Flatten each ball with the bottom of a glass dipped in cold water. Press the nutmeats into the tops of the cookies. Wrap each individually in waxed paper. Refrigerate or freeze. Yields 5 dozen cookies.

DATE COOKIES

½ cup honey
2 eggs
1 teaspoon vanilla extract
1 teaspoon lemon juice
2 cups dates, pitted
2 cups English walnuts

Blend together the honey, eggs, vanilla, and lemon juice. Grind the dates and walnuts in a meat grinder. Combine the two mixtures, and shape into balls the size of a walnut. Place the balls on greased cooky sheets. Flatten each with the bottom of a glass dipped in cold water. Bake at 350° F. for 10 to 12 minutes. Yields 4 dozen cookies.

RAISIN COOKIES

3 tablespoons honey
3 tablespoons unsulfured molasses
1 tablespoon blackstrap molasses
1 tablespoon oil
2 eggs
1½ cups wheat germ
⅓ cup soy flour
¾ cup sunflower seed meal
½ cup raisins, steamed

Blend all the ingredients together, in the order given, and mix thoroughly. Drop by tablespoonfuls onto greased cooky sheets. Bake at 350° F. for 10 to 12 minutes. Yields 3 dozen cookies.

RAISIN-SPICE COOKIES

2 cups raisins
1 cup boiling water
2½ cups honey
1 cup oil
3 eggs
1 teaspoon vanilla extract
4 cups wholewheat flour
1½ teaspoons allspice, ground
1½ teaspoons cinnamon, ground
½ teaspoon nutmeg, grated
1 cup nutmeats, broken

Soak the raisins in the hot water for ½ hour. Blend the honey, oil, eggs, and vanilla. To this mixture, add the flour, spices, and raisins. Blend thoroughly. Add the nutmeats. Chill. Drop by teaspoonfuls onto greased, floured cooky sheets. Bake at 400° F. for 10 to 15 minutes. Yields 5 dozen cookies.

APPLESAUCE COOKIES

1 cup honey
1 cup oil
2 eggs
¼ cup blackstrap molasses
1 cup applesauce
2½ cups wholewheat flour
½ cup millet flour
2 tablespoons cinnamon, ground
½ cup sunflower seeds, whole
1 cup raisins, steamed

Blend all the ingredients in the order given. Drop by teaspoonfuls onto greased cooky sheets. Bake at 375° F. for 15 minutes. Yields 6 dozen cookies.

COTTAGE CHEESE COOKIES

1 cup butter
1 cup cottage cheese, drained
1 egg yolk
⅓ cup honey
2 cups oat flour (about)
1 egg white
⅓ cup sesame seed meal
1 teaspoon cinnamon, ground

Blend the butter and cottage cheese together. Add the egg yolk and honey. Mix thoroughly. Add enough oat flour to make the dough a good consistency to hold together. Chill the dough for 1 hour. Roll it to ⅛-inch thickness on a lightly floured board. Cut into shapes. Place on greased cooky sheets. Brush with egg white, and top with sesame seed meal and cinnamon, which have been mixed together. Bake at 350° F. for 12 to 15 minutes, or until brown and crisp. Yields 5 dozen cookies.

CARROT-MOLASSES COOKIES

½ cup unsulfured molasses
2 tablespoons oil
1 cup raw carrots, grated
2 cups graham flour
½ teaspoon nutmeg, grated
½ teaspoon cinnamon, ground
1 cup nutmeats, broken
1 cup dates, pitted and cut
1 cup warm water

Blend together the molasses, oil, carrots, graham flour, nutmeg, cinnamon, and nutmeats. Blend the dates and warm water in an electric blender, and pour this mixture over the first mixture. Mix thoroughly, and drop by teaspoonfuls onto greased cooky sheets. Bake at 350° F. for 12 to 15 minutes. Yields 6 dozen cookies.

PEANUT BUTTER COOKIES

1 cup honey
$\frac{2}{3}$ cup oil
1 cup peanut butter
2 eggs, beaten
$2\frac{1}{2}$ cups wholewheat flour

Blend all the ingredients together thoroughly, and drop by teaspoonfuls onto greased cooky sheets. Bake at 350° F. for 10 to 12 minutes. Yields 7 dozen cookies.

PEANUT BUTTER–OATMEAL COOKIES

1½ cups honey
½ cup peanut butter
½ cup milk
1 teaspoon vanilla extract
2 tablespoons brewer's yeast
2 teaspoons bone meal
3 cups rolled oats, lightly toasted in the oven

Blend in a saucepan the honey, peanut butter, and milk. Bring to a boil over gentle heat. Combine with the remaining ingredients, and mix thoroughly. Drop by teaspoonfuls onto cold plates. Chill. Wrap individually in waxed paper. Refrigerate. Yields 6 dozen cookies.

PECAN COOKIES

1 cup maple syrup
1 cup oil
2 eggs, beaten
2 teaspoons vanilla extract
2 cups pecans, broken
3 cups oat flour (about)

Blend all the ingredients, in the order given, adding only enough oat flour to make the dough a good consistency to drop by teaspoonfuls onto greased cooky sheets. Bake at 350° F. for 15 to 20 minutes. Yields 6 to 7 dozen cookies.

ALMOND COOKIES

½ cup date sugar
⅓ cup honey
⅔ cup oil
2 eggs
1 teaspoon cinnamon, ground
1⅓ cups almonds, blanched and ground
3 cups oat flour (about)

Blend all the ingredients, in the order given, adding only enough oat flour to make the dough a good consistency to hold together. Shape into two long rolls, about 1½ inches in thickness. Chill overnight. Cut into slices ¼-inch thick. Place the slices on greased cooky sheets. Bake at 400° F. for 8 to 10 minutes. Yields 6 dozen cookies.

SUNFLOWER SEED COOKIES

- 1½ cups honey
- 1 cup oil
- 2 eggs
- 1 cup sunflower seed meal
- 3 cups rolled oats, uncooked
- ¾ cup oat flour (about)
- 1 teaspoon nutmeg, grated
- 1 cup raisins, steamed

Blend all the ingredients together, adding only enough oat flour to make the dough a good consistency to hold together. Shape the dough into long rolls, wrap in waxed paper, and refrigerate overnight. Cut into ¼-inch-thick slices and place on greased cooky sheets. Bake at 375° F. for 8 to 10 minutes. Yields 7 to 7½ dozen cookies.

NUT-SEED-FRUIT COOKIES

1½ cups dried fruits, cut in small pieces
1 cup hot water
1 cup honey
½ cup oil
2 cups graham flour
1 cup sunflower seed meal
1½ cups nutmeats, broken

Soak the dried fruits in the hot water for 10 minutes, and then purée them in an electric blender. Meantime, mix together thoroughly the honey, oil, graham flour, sunflower seed meal, and nutmeats. Combine the two mixtures, stir together thoroughly, and drop by teaspoonfuls onto greased cooky sheets. Flatten with the tines of a fork to form 1½-inch cookies. Bake at 350° F. for 15 minutes. Yields 7 dozen cookies.

CARDAMOM SEED COOKIES

- ¼ cup honey
- ¾ cup date sugar, firmly packed
- ⅓ cup oil
- ¼ cup water
- 1 teaspoon cardamom seeds, ground
- 1 cup cashews, ground
- 1½ cups rolled oats, uncooked
- ½ cup oat flour (about)

Blend all the ingredients, in the order given, adding only enough oat flour to make the dough a good consistency to drop by teaspoonfuls onto greased cooky sheets. Flatten each cooky with the bottom of a glass dipped in cold water. Bake at 350° F. for 12 to 15 minutes. Yields 5 dozen cookies.

POPPY SEED COOKIES

½ cup honey
⅔ cup oil
2 eggs
1 teaspoon vanilla extract
½ cup milk
2 tablespoons grated orange rind, from organic fruit
1 cup poppy seeds
¼ cup nonfat dry milk powder
2½ cups oat flour

Blend all the ingredients together, forming a fairly thin dough. Drop by the teaspoonful onto greased cooky sheets, allowing space between the cookies. Bake at 350° F. for 8 to 10 minutes, or until golden brown on the edges. Yields 7 dozen cookies.

ENRICHED COOKIES

1 cup honey
½ cup oil
4 egg yolks
½ cup water
1 cup rolled oats, uncooked
1 cup wholewheat flour
1 cup wheat germ
¼ cup brewer's yeast
¼ cup bone meal
½ cup nonfat dry milk powder
½ teaspoon cinnamon, ground
½ teaspoon nutmeg, grated
4 egg whites, stiffly beaten

Blend together the honey, oil, egg yolks and water. Add all the dry ingredients, and mix thoroughly. Fold in the stiffly beaten egg whites, and drop by the teaspoonful onto greased cooky sheets. Bake at 350° F. for 25 to 30 minutes. Yields 6 dozen cookies.

FORTIFIED COOKIES

3 tablespoons unsulfured molasses
1 cup oil
2 eggs
1 teaspoon vanilla extract
2 cups oat flour
¼ cup soy flour
1 tablespoon wheat germ
3 tablespoons nonfat dry milk powder

Blend all the ingredients together. Drop by teaspoonfuls onto greased cooky sheets. Flatten each cooky with the bottom of a glass dipped in cold water. Bake at 375° F. for 12 to 15 minutes. Yields 2 to 2½ dozen cookies.

CAROB-BUTTERMILK COOKIES

1 cup honey
½ cup oil
2 eggs
1 cup buttermilk
1 teaspoon vanilla extract
1½ cups rolled oats, uncooked
2½ cups oat flour
½ cup carob powder
1 cup nutmeats, broken

Blend together thoroughly the honey, oil, eggs, buttermilk, and vanilla. Add the remainder of the ingredients, and mix well. Drop by teaspoonfuls onto greased cooky sheets. Bake at 375° F. for 12 to 15 minutes. Yields 7 dozen cookies.

MAPLE SYRUP COOKIES

1 cup maple syrup
1 cup oil
2 eggs
2 cups rolled oats, uncooked
1½ cups wholewheat flour (about)
½ cup nutmeats, broken

Blend together thoroughly the maple syrup, oil, and eggs. Add the remainder of the ingredients, using only enough flour to make the dough firm. Divide the dough in half, and roll into 2 rolls about 2 inches in diameter. Chill for at least 2 hours. Slice to about ½-inch thickness, and place on greased cooky sheets. Bake at 350° F. for 12 to 15 minutes. Yields 7 dozen cookies.

LEMON COOKIES

- ¾ cup date sugar, packed firmly
- ⅓ cup oil
- ¼ cup water
- ¼ cup lemon juice
- ½ teaspoon grated lemon rind, from organic fruit
- 1 cup cashews, ground
- 2 cups oat flour (about)

Blend all the ingredients, in the order given, adding only enough oat flour to make the dough a good consistency to drop by teaspoonfuls onto greased cooky sheets. Flatten each cooky with the bottom of a glass dipped in cold water. Bake at 350° F. for 12 to 15 minutes. Yields 5 dozen cookies.

VANILLA COOKIES

½ cup honey
1 cup oil
2 eggs
2 teaspoons vanilla extract
1½ cups oat flour (about)

Blend all the ingredients, adding only enough oat flour to make the dough a good consistency to drop by teaspoonfuls onto greased cooky sheets. Space the dough 1 inch apart. Bake at 350° F. for 7 to 10 minutes, or until the edges of the cookies are brown. Yields 3 dozen cookies.

UNBAKED PATTIES

3 cups rolled oats, uncooked
½ cup milk
½ cup oil
½ cup peanut butter
½ cup carob powder
1 cup honey

Soak the oats for 1 hour in the milk and oil combined. Add the remaining ingredients, and blend thoroughly. Shape into small balls the size of a walnut, and flatten them between your palms. Wrap the patties individually in waxed paper. Refrigerate. Yields 4 dozen patties.

FLOURLESS COOKIES
(in electric blender)

¼ cup honey
¼ cup oil
4 eggs
½ cup orange juice
1½ cups English walnuts
1½ cups wheat germ (about)

Blend together in an electric blender the honey, oil, eggs, orange juice, and walnuts. Pour into a bowl, and add only enough wheat germ to make it a good consistency to hold together. Drop by teaspoonfuls onto greased cooky sheets. Bake at 300° F. for 8 to 10 minutes. Yields 4 dozen cookies.

Squares and Bars

WHEAT GERM SQUARES

1 cup honey
2 eggs
¼ cup carob powder
2 teaspoons vanilla extract
2 cups wheat germ

Blend all the ingredients thoroughly, and turn into 2 greased 8x8x2-inch pans. Bake at 350° F. for 15 or 20 minutes. Although it may look soft, it becomes firm as it cools. Score into 2x2-inch squares immediately, but do not remove the squares from the pans until they cool. Yields 32 squares.

FOUR-GRAIN SQUARES

1 cup honey
1 cup oil
2 eggs
¾ cup corn flour
¾ cup millet flour
¾ cup oat flour
¾ cup soy flour
1 teaspoon mace, ground
1 teaspoon cinnamon, ground
1 teaspoon almond extract

Blend the honey and the oil. Beat in the eggs. Sift the flours and spices together, and add them to the liquid mixture. Add the almond extract. Blend thoroughly. Chill the dough 1 hour. Turn into 2 greased 8x8x2-inch pans. Bake at 375° F. for 15 minutes. Cool, and cut into 2x2-inch squares. Yields 32 squares.

OATMEAL-COCONUT SQUARES

- 1 cup honey
- 1 cup oil
- 2 eggs
- 1 teaspoon almond extract
- 2 cups rolled oats, uncooked
- ½ cup wholewheat flour (about)

Blend together thoroughly the honey, oil, eggs, and almond extract. Add the rolled oats and only enough wholewheat flour to make the dough a good consistency to turn into 2 greased 8x8x2-inch pans. Bake at 350° F. for 25 to 30 minutes, or until golden brown. Cool in the pans. Then cut into 2x2-inch squares. Yields 32 squares.

RYE-OATMEAL SQUARES

1 cup honey
1 cup oil
2 egg yolks
1 teaspoon vanilla extract
½ cup nutmeats, broken
½ cup soy grits
1 cup rolled oats, uncooked
1 cup rye flour
2 egg whites
1 teaspoon honey

Blend together all the ingredients, except the egg whites and 1 teaspoon honey. Mix thoroughly. Turn the batter into 2 greased 8x8x2-inch pans. Beat the egg whites until stiff, adding 1 teaspoonful of honey as they begin to stiffen. Spread the egg white mixture over the top of the batter. Bake at 350° F. for 15 to 18 minutes, or until the egg white is golden brown and the batter is baked. Allow to cool for 5 minutes. Then score into 2x2-inch squares with a sharp knife. Yields 32 squares.

HONEY-MOLASSES SQUARES

½ cup honey
1 cup unsulfured molasses
1 cup oil
1 teaspoon vanilla extract
2 cups wholewheat flour
1 cup rolled oats, uncooked
1 cup soy flour
1 cup dried coconut shreds, unsweetened

Blend together thoroughly the honey, molasses, oil, and vanilla. Add the wholewheat flour, rolled oats, soy flour, and half the coconut shreds. Mix well. Turn the batter into 2 greased 8x8x2-inch pans. Strew the remaining coconut shreds on top of the batter. Bake at 350° F. for 15 to 20 minutes. Cut into 2x2-inch squares. Yields 32 squares.

ANISE SQUARES

1⅓ cups honey
½ cup oil
3 eggs
2 teaspoons anise seeds
3 cups oat flour (about)
½ cup blanched almonds

Blend the honey and the oil. Add the eggs, one at a time, beating thoroughly after each addition. Add the anise seeds and enough oat flour to make the dough a good consistency to hold together. Press the dough into a greased 12x8x2-inch pan, and pat it firmly until smooth on top. Score the top into 2-inch squares, using a sharp knife. Press a whole almond into the center of each square. Bake at 350° F. for 15 to 20 minutes. Yields 24 squares.

UNCOOKED APRICOT SQUARES

1½ cups dried unsulfured apricots
1½ cups fresh coconut pieces
1½ cups nutmeats
1 tablespoon grated orange rind, from organic fruit
1 tablespoon grated lemon rind, from organic fruit

Grind together in a meat grinder the apricots, coconut, and nutmeats. Combine with the orange and lemon rinds, and blend well. Turn the mixture into 2 greased and floured 8x8x2-inch pans. Refrigerate. Since these squares are a confection, they can be cut quite small. Cut into 1x1-inch squares, and wrap each individually in waxed paper. Refrigerate. Yields 10⅔ dozen squares.

UNCOOKED PEANUT BUTTER SQUARES

2 cups peanut butter
¾ cup honey
2 teaspoons vanilla extract
1½ cups dried coconut shreds, unsweetened
2 tablespoons bone meal
½ cup sunflower seed meal
½ cup nonfat dry milk powder
1 cup wheat germ
1 cup peanuts, ground
water

Blend all the ingredients together thoroughly, adding only enough water to make the dough a good consistency to hold together. Pat the dough into 2 greased 8x8x2-inch pans. Chill. Cut into 2x2-inch squares. Yields 32 squares.

UNCOOKED CAROB BROWNIES

- 2 tablespoons honey
- 2 tablespoons oil
- 2 teaspoons vanilla extract
- 1 cup carob powder
- 1 cup wheat germ
- 1 cup soy lecithin
- 1 cup English walnuts, chopped
- ½ cup sesame seed meal
- ½ cup sunflower seed meal
- 1 cup milk (about)
- ½ cup dried coconut shreds, unsweetened

Blend together the honey, oil, vanilla, carob powder, wheat germ, soy lecithin, walnuts, sesame seed meal, and sunflower seed meal. Then add enough milk to make the dough a good consistency to hold together. Pat the dough into a greased 8x8x2-inch pan. Strew the coconut shreds on top of the dough. Refrigerate. Cut into 1x1-inch squares. Yields 5⅓ dozen brownies.

UNCOOKED CAROB-NUT SQUARES

1 cup honey
1 cup oil
2 teaspoons vanilla extract
1 cup carob powder
½ cup nutmeats, ground
1½ cups nonfat dry milk powder.

Blend all the ingredients together thoroughly, and pat into 2 greased 8x8x2-inch pans. Chill overnight. Because these squares are a confection, they can be cut quite small. Cut into 1x1-inch squares, and wrap each individually in waxed paper. Refrigerate or freeze. Yields 10⅔ dozen squares.

JIFFY CAROB SQUARES

⅔ cup honey
⅔ cup oil
2 eggs
¼ cup light cream
1 teaspoon vanilla extract
½ cup carob powder
1 cup oat flour (about)
1 cup nutmeats, broken

Blend together all the ingredients except the oat flour and nutmeats. Then add enough oat flour to give the dough a good consistency for pouring into 2 greased 8x8x2-inch pans. Sprinkle the nutmeats over the top. Bake at 400° F. for 10 to 12 minutes. Cut into 2x2-inch squares while warm. Yields 32 squares.

POPPY SEED–CAROB SQUARES

1 cup honey
1 cup oil
1 cup hot milk
2 cups poppy seeds
½ cup carob powder
1 teaspoon cinnamon, ground
½ teaspoon cloves, ground
2½ cups oat flour

Blend all the ingredients together. Pour the dough into 2 greased 8x8x2-inch pans. Bake at 350° F. for 25 to 30 minutes. Cool, and cut into 2x2-inch squares. Yields 32 squares.

Note: This batter will also make good cookies. Drop the batter by the teaspoonful onto greased cooky sheets. Flatten gently, with the tips of your fingers, to form cookies ¼-inch thick and 1½ inches in diameter. Bake at 350° F. for 10 to 12 minutes. The cookies will become crisp as they cool. Yields 12 dozen cookies.

WHEAT GERM–CAROB BROWNIES

1½ cups honey
2 tablespoons unsulfured molasses
¼ cup oil
4 eggs, beaten
2 teaspoons vanilla extract
1 teaspoon cinnamon, ground
½ cup carob powder
1 cup nonfat dry milk powder
2 cups wheat germ
1 cup nutmeats, broken
1 cup wholewheat flour (about)

Blend together all the ingredients, in the order given, using only enough wholewheat flour to make the dough a good consistency to hold together. Turn the dough into 2 greased and floured 8x8x2-inch pans. Bake at 350° F. for 30 to 35 minutes. Cut into 2x2-inch squares. Yields 2⅔ dozen squares.

HONEY-CAROB BROWNIES

- 1⅓ cups honey
- 1 cup oil
- 4 eggs
- 2 teaspoons vanilla extract
- 1 cup carob powder
- 1 cup nutmeats, broken
- 2 cups wholewheat flour (about)

Blend all the ingredients, in the order given, adding only enough wholewheat flour to make a dough of a consistency to hold together. Turn the dough into 2 greased 8x8x2-inch pans. Bake at 350° F. for 25 to 30 minutes. Cut into 2x2-inch squares. Yields 2⅔ dozen brownies.

SESAME-CAROB BROWNIES

1½ cups carob syrup
1 cup oil
4 eggs, beaten
¼ cup lemon juice
2 teaspoons vanilla extract
½ teaspoon sea salt
1⅓ cups carob powder
1 cup sesame seeds
2½ cups wholewheat flour (about)

Blend together the carob syrup, oil, eggs, lemon juice, vanilla, salt, and carob powder. Add to this mixture ½ cup of the sesame seeds, and enough of the wholewheat flour to make a dough of a good consistency to hold together. Turn the dough into 2 greased 8x8x2-inch pans. Sprinkle the top with the remaining ½ cup of sesame seeds. Bake at 350° F. for 25 to 30 minutes. Cut into 2x2-inch squares. Yields 2⅔ dozen squares.

ALMOND-CAROB BROWNIES

1 cup carob syrup
1 cup oil
1 cup carob powder
4 eggs, beaten
2 teaspoons almond extract
½ teaspoon sea salt
1 cup soy lecithin
1 cup almonds (reserve 32 whole, and grind the remainder)
4 cups wholewheat flour (about)

Blend together the carob syrup, oil, carob powder, eggs, almond extract, salt, and soy lecithin. Add the ground almonds and enough wholewheat flour to make a dough of a good consistency to hold together. Turn the dough into 2 greased 8x8x2-inch pans. Press the whole almonds into the top of the batter, so that they are evenly spaced 4 across and 4 down. Bake at 350° F. for 25 to 30 minutes. Cut into 2x2-inch squares, with an almond in the center of each square. Yields 2⅔ dozen squares.

MOLASSES-CAROB BROWNIES

- ½ cup unsulfured molasses
- ¼ cup blackstrap molasses
- ¼ cup date sugar, firmly packed
- ½ cup oil
- 1 egg
- ¼ cup carob powder
- ½ cup soy flour
- 1 cup nutmeats, broken
- ½ cup wholewheat flour (about)

Blend all the ingredients, in the order given, adding only enough wholewheat flour to make a dough of a good consistency to hold together. Turn the dough into a greased and floured 12x8x2-inch pan. Bake at 275° F. for 30 to 40 minutes. Cut into 2x2-inch squares. Yields 2 dozen brownies.

SOY-CAROB BROWNIES

2 cups date sugar, firmly packed
1 cup oil
2 teaspoons vanilla extract
2 egg yolks, beaten
½ cup soy flour
½ cup oat flour
½ cup carob powder
1 cup nutmeats, broken
2 egg whites, stiffly beaten

Blend the date sugar and the oil. Add the vanilla and the beaten egg yolks. Mix thoroughly. Add the flours, carob powder, and nutmeats. Then fold in the stiffly beaten egg whites. Turn the mixture into 2 greased and floured 8x8x2-inch pans. Bake at 350° F. for 20 to 30 minutes. Cut into 2x2-inch squares. Yields 2⅔ dozen brownies.

RYE-OATMEAL BARS

1 cup honey
1 cup oil
2 egg yolks
1 teaspoon vanilla extract
1 cup rye flour
1 cup rolled oats, uncooked
2 egg whites, stiffly beaten
¼ cup sesame seeds

Blend the honey, oil, egg yolks, and vanilla. Add to this mixture the rye flour and rolled oats. Mix thoroughly. Then fold in the stiffly beaten egg whites. Pour the dough into a greased 12x8x2-inch pan. Sprinkle the top of it with sesame seeds. Bake at 350° F. for 30 to 35 minutes. Cut into 1x4-inch bars. Remove the bars from the pan while still warm. Yields 2 dozen bars.

COCONUT–WHEAT GERM BARS

½ cup honey
⅓ cup oil
3 eggs, beaten
2 teaspoons lemon extract
1 cup wheat germ
2 cups dried coconut shreds, unsweetened
1 cup raisins, steamed

Blend together thoroughly the honey, oil, eggs, and lemon extract. Add to this mixture the wheat germ, coconut shreds, and raisins. Mix thoroughly. Pour the dough into a greased 12x8x2-inch pan. Bake at 325° F. from 25 to 30 minutes. Cut into 1x4-inch bars while still warm. Yields 2 dozen bars.

BANANA-WALNUT BARS

2 tablespoons dry yeast granules
¼ cup warm water
1½ cups honey
1 cup oil
4 eggs
2 teaspoons vanilla extract
2 cups banana, mashed
3 cups wholewheat flour
¼ cup soy flour
2 cups English walnuts, broken

Soften the yeast in the water. When the mixture bubbles, add the honey and oil, and blend thoroughly. Add the eggs, one at a time, beating well after each addition. Add the remaining ingredients, and mix well. Turn the batter into 3 greased 8x8x2-inch pans. Set the batter in a warm place for 1½ to 2 hours, or until it has risen to almost double in bulk. Bake at 350° F. for 30 to 35 minutes. Allow to cool. Then cut into 1x4-inch bars. Yields 4 dozen bars.

APRICOT BARS

1 cup dry unsulfured apricots
1 cup hot water
1 cup date sugar, firmly packed
¼ cup oil
¼ cup arrowroot flour
½ cup nonfat dry milk powder
1 cup oat flour (about)

Cut the apricots into small pieces and soak them for 1 hour in the hot water. Put the mixture in an electric blender, and blend thoroughly. Put the resulting pulp in a bowl. Add the remaining ingredients, using only enough oat flour to make a batter of good consistency to turn into a greased 12x8x2-inch pan. Bake at 375° F. for 20 to 25 minutes. Cut into 4x1-inch bars. Yields 2 dozen bars.

FRUIT BARS

1⅓ cups malt syrup
½ cup oil
4 eggs
1 teaspoon vanilla extract
2 cups pitted dates, chopped
1 cup soy grits
1 cup wheat germ
1½ cups oat flour (about)

Combine all the ingredients, adding only enough oat flour to make a dough of a good consistency to hold together. Turn the dough into 2 greased 12x8x2-inch pans. Bake at 350° F. for 20 to 25 minutes. Cut into 4x1-inch bars while still warm. Yields 4 dozen bars.

FRUIT-FILLED BARS

DOUGH:

¾ cup honey
¾ cup oil
2 cups wholewheat flour
2 cups rolled oats, uncooked

Blend all the ingredients together until they form a crumb mixture. Press ½ of the mixture into a greased 12x8x2-inch pan.

FILLING:

½ cup honey
3 tablespoons arrowroot flour
½ cup warm water
2 tablespoons lemon juice
2½ cups dried raisins and dates, ground

Place all the ingredients in a saucepan. Cook over a low heat, stirring constantly, until the mixture thickens. Cool, and pour over the crumb mixture in the pan. Cover this filling with the remaining crumb mixture. Bake at 400° F. from 20 to 30 minutes. When partly cooled, cut into 1x4-inch bars. Yields 2 dozen bars.

NUT-FRUIT BARS

3 tablespoons honey
½ cup oil
2 cups pitted dates, ground
⅔ cup nutmeats, broken
½ cup sesame seeds
½ cup dried coconut shreds, unsweetened
⅔ cup milk
1 teaspoon lemon extract
2 cups wholewheat flour
2 cups oat flour (about)

Blend all the ingredients, in the order given, adding only enough oat flour to make a dough of a good consistency to hold together. Turn the dough into 2 greased 8x8x2-inch pans, and press firmly until smooth. Bake at 375° F. for 20 to 25 minutes, or until browned. Cut into 4x1-inch bars. Yields 2⅔ dozen bars.

NUT BARS

¾ cup honey
1 cup oil
1 egg
1 teaspoon cinnamon, ground
3 cups oat flour
½ cup nutmeats, broken

Blend all the ingredients together, and turn the batter into a greased 12x8x2-inch pan. Bake at 350° F. for 20 to 25 minutes, or until lightly browned. Cool, and score into 4x1-inch bars. Remove gently. Yields 2 dozen bars.

PECAN-MOLASSES BARS

½ cup unsulfured molasses
2 tablespoons blackstrap molasses
⅓ cup date sugar, firmly packed
⅔ cup oil
4 cups rolled oats, uncooked
2 teaspoons vanilla extract
1 cup pecans, broken

Blend together thoroughly the unsulfured molasses, blackstrap molasses, date sugar, oil, rolled oats, and vanilla. Pour the batter into 2 greased and floured 8x8x2-inch pans. Sprinkle the pecans over the top of the batter. Bake at 350° F. for 10 to 15 minutes, or until browned. Cut into 4x1-inch bars. Yields 2⅔ dozen bars.

Rolled Balls

PEANUT BUTTER–WHEAT GERM BALLS

½ cup honey
½ cup date sugar, firmly packed
½ cup oil
1 egg
½ cup peanut butter
¼ cup wheat germ
1¾ cups oat flour (about)

Blend all the ingredients together, in the order given, using only enough oat flour to make a dough of a good consistency to hold together. Shape the dough into small balls, the size of a walnut. Place the balls on greased cooky sheets. Bake at 350° F. for 8 to 10 minutes. Yields 4 dozen balls.

DATE-CASHEW BALLS

$\frac{2}{3}$ cup honey
$\frac{2}{3}$ cup oil
$\frac{1}{3}$ cup water
2 teaspoons vanilla extract
2 cups pitted dates, ground
2 cups raw cashews, ground
2 cups rolled oats, uncooked
2 cups oat flour (about)

Blend all the ingredients together, in the order given, adding only enough oat flour to make a dough of a good consistency to hold together. Shape the dough into small balls, the size of a walnut. Place on greased cooky sheets. Bake at 350° F. for 12 to 15 minutes. Yields 7 to 8 dozen balls.

PECAN BALLS

¼ cup honey
1 cup oil
2 teaspoons vanilla extract
2 cups pecans, ground
2 cups oat flour (about)
1 tablespoon cinnamon, ground

Blend together the honey, oil, vanilla, and pecans. Add to this mixture enough oat flour to make a dough of a good consistency to hold together. Chill. Shape the dough into small balls, the size of a walnut. Place the balls on greased cooky sheets. Bake at 325° F. for 25 to 30 minutes. Remove from the oven, and dust immediately with the cinnamon. Yields 6 dozen balls.

COCONUT BALLS

4 egg whites
¾ cup honey
½ teaspoon lemon extract
¾ cup raw cashews, broken
2 cups wheat germ
1 cup dried coconut shreds, unsweetened

Beat the egg whites until very stiff. Continue the beating while gradually adding the honey, a bit at a time. Add the lemon extract, and fold in the remaining ingredients. Drop the mixture by tablespoonfuls onto greased and floured cooky sheets. Bake at 300° F. for 10 to 12 minutes. Yields 3 dozen balls.

POPCORN BALLS

1 cup honey
$\frac{1}{2}$ cup hot water
1 tablespoon cider vinegar
1 tablespoon oil
2 tablespoons blackstrap molasses
6 cups popped corn

Place in a saucepan the honey, hot water, and vinegar. Bring to a boil over a gentle heat, and simmer for 5 minutes. Add the oil and molasses, and continue to cook the mixture gently until a teaspoonful of it forms a ball when dropped into cold water. Remove the mixture from the heat, and cool it slightly. Pour it over freshly popped corn. Dip your hands in cold water, and form popcorn balls the size of plums. Yields 24 balls.

CARDAMOM BALLS

$1\frac{3}{4}$ cups honey
1 cup softened butter
2 eggs
2 teaspoons cardamom seeds, ground
2 teaspoons cinnamon, ground
3 cups oat flour (about)

Blend the ingredients, in the order given, adding only enough oat flour to make a dough of a good consistency to hold together. Roll the dough into small balls, the size of a walnut. Place the balls on greased, floured cooky sheets. Bake at 350° F. for 8 to 10 minutes, or until lightly browned. Yields 6 dozen balls.

GOLDEN BALLS

$1\frac{1}{3}$ cups honey
$1\frac{1}{4}$ cups oil
3 eggs
$\frac{1}{2}$ teaspoon almond extract
$\frac{1}{4}$ cup grated orange rind, from organic fruit
$3\frac{1}{4}$ cups oat flour (about)

Blend the honey and the oil. Add the eggs, one at a time, beating the mixture well after each addition. Add the remaining ingredients, using only enough oat flour to make a firm dough. Shape the dough into small balls, the size of a walnut, and place on greased cooky sheets. Bake at 400° F. for 15 minutes. Yields 4 dozen balls.

SPICE BALLS

- ½ cup softened butter
- ⅓ cup honey
- 1 teaspoon vanilla extract
- ¾ cup sunflower seed meal
- ¾ cup sesame seed meal
- 1 teaspoon nutmeg, grated
- 1 teaspoon cinnamon, ground
- 2 cups oat flour (about)

Blend the butter and the honey. Add the rest of the ingredients, using only enough flour to make a dough of a good consistency to hold together. Shape the dough into small balls, the size of a walnut. Place on greased cooky sheets. Bake at 300° F. for 12 to 15 minutes. Yields 5 to 6 dozen balls.

UNCOOKED WHEAT GERM–SUNFLOWER SEED BALLS

¾ cup wheat germ
½ cup sunflower seeds, ground
⅔ cup peanut butter
½ cup honey
1 teaspoon unsulfured molasses
2 tablespoons dried coconut shreds, unsweetened
½ cup nonfat dry milk powder
additional sunflower seeds, ground

Blend together thoroughly all the ingredients listed except the last. Shape the mixture into small balls, the size of a walnut. Roll the balls in the additional ground sunflower seeds. Refrigerate. Yields 4 to 5 dozen balls.

UNCOOKED SPROUTED WHEAT BALLS

⅓ cup wholewheat berries, sprouted
1 cup pitted dates
½ cup nutmeats
2 apples, peeled and quartered
1 teaspoon lemon extract
¼ cup dried coconut shreds, unsweetened

Soak the wholewheat berries overnight in water. In the morning, drain them. Rinse the berries twice a day, keeping them moist but not standing in water. By the third day, the grains will have sprouted sufficiently to use. Combine them with the dates, nutmeats, and apples. Grind this mixture in a meat grinder. Then add the lemon extract. Shape the mixture into small balls, the size of a walnut. Roll the balls in coconut shreds. Refrigerate. Yields 4 dozen balls.

UNCOOKED HONEY-NUT BALLS

1 cup honey
1 cup wheat germ
1 cup peanut butter
½ cup sunflower seeds, ground
½ cup nutmeats, ground
½ cup whey powder
½ cup nonfat dry milk powder

Blend together thoroughly all the ingredients listed except the last. Shape the mixture into small balls, the size of a walnut. Roll the balls in the dry milk powder. Refrigerate. Yields 5 to 6 dozen balls.

UNCOOKED FRUIT BALLS

1 cup pitted dates
1 cup figs
1 cup unsulfured dried apricots
1 cup dried peaches
1 cup raisins
1 cup currants
½ cup dried coconut shreds, unsweetened

Grind together in a meat grinder all the ingredients listed except the last. Blend the mixture thoroughly. Shape into little balls, the size of a walnut. Roll the balls in the coconut shreds. Refrigerate. Yields 8 to 9 dozen balls.

UNCOOKED PEANUT BUTTER BALLS

½ cup honey
1 cup peanut butter
¼ cup sesame seeds
¼ cup soy lecithin
3 tablespoons brewer's yeast
1 teaspoon bone meal
¼ cup dried coconut shreds, unsweetened

Blend together thoroughly all the ingredients listed except the last. Shape the mixture into small balls, the size of a walnut. Roll the balls in the coconut shreds. Refrigerate. Yields 3 dozen balls.

UNCOOKED SESAME SEED BALLS

1 cup wheat germ
1½ cups sesame seeds, ground
½ cup brewer's yeast
2 cups dried coconut shreds, unsweetened
½ cup warmed honey (about)
additional sesame seeds, whole

Blend together the wheat germ, sesame seeds, yeast, and coconut shreds. Add enough honey to the mixture to bind it together. Shape the mixture into small balls, the size of a walnut. Roll the balls in the whole sesame seeds. Refrigerate. Yields 5 to 6 dozen balls.

UNCOOKED SEED-NUT BALLS

1 cup sunflower seeds
1 cup pumpkin seeds
1 cup sesame seeds
1 cup nutmeats
1 cup dried coconut shreds, unsweetened
½ cup carob powder
1 cup date sugar
water

Grind the seeds and the nutmeats in an electric seed grinder. Turn this meal into a bowl. Add to it the coconut shreds, carob powder, and date sugar. Stir this mixture until well blended, and add only enough water to bind it together. Shape the mixture into small balls, the size of a walnut. Refrigerate. Yields 6 to 7 dozen balls.

UNCOOKED FORTIFIED BALLS

1 cup wheat germ
½ cup rice polish
2 tablespoons rose hip powder
10 tablespoons whey powder
1 tablespoon bone meal
10 tablespoons brewer's yeast
½ cup oil
1 teaspoon kelp
1 tablespoon blackstrap molasses
1 cup pitted dates, chopped
1 cup dried coconut shreds, unsweetened
1 cup nutmeats, ground
1 cup raisins
½ cup honey

Blend all the ingredients together thoroughly. Shape into little balls, the size of a walnut. Refrigerate. Yields 7 to 8 dozen balls.

Thin Wafers, Chunky Rocks

ROLLED OAT WAFERS

¾ cup honey
⅓ cup oil
1 egg, beaten
3 tablespoons milk
½ teaspoon nutmeg, grated
1 teaspoon cinnamon, ground
1 cup rolled oats, uncooked
½ cup raisins, steamed
½ cup nutmeats, broken
1 cup oat flour (about)

Blend all the ingredients, in the order given, adding enough oat flour to make a dough of a good consistency to drop by the teaspoonful onto greased cooky sheets, about 2½ inches apart. Flatten each wafer with the bottom of a glass dipped in cold water. Bake at 350° F. for 8 to 10 minutes. While the wafers are still warm, roll them over the handle of a wooden spoon. If the cookies become too crisp to roll, soften them by returning them to the warm oven for a minute or two. Yields 3 dozen wafers.

TAPIOCA FLOUR WAFERS

These wafers have a delicate flavor, somewhat reminiscent of ladyfingers.

1 cup honey
1 cup oil
2 eggs
½ cup sesame seeds
2 cups tapioca flour
½ teaspoon ginger, ground

Blend all the ingredients together thoroughly. The batter will be quite thin. Drop it by the ½ teaspoonful onto greased cooky sheets, allowing ample room for the wafers to spread. Bake at 350° F. for 10 to 12 minutes. Yields 7 dozen thin wafers of 2½-inch diameter.

ARROWROOT FLOUR WAFERS

1 cup honey
1 cup oil
2 cups arrowroot flour
2 eggs
2 teaspoons almond extract
1 cup dried coconut shreds, unsweetened

Blend all the ingredients together thoroughly, making a thin batter. Drop the batter by the ½ teaspoonful onto greased cooky sheets, allowing ample room for the batter to spread. Bake at 350° F. for 8 to 10 minutes. Carefully and immediately remove the wafers from the cooky sheets with a spatula. Yields 7 dozen thin, crisp wafers.

ALMOND WAFERS

¾ cup honey
½ cup oil
½ cup milk
½ cup almonds, ground
2 cups oat flour (about)
2 teaspoons cinnamon, ground

Blend together the honey, oil, milk, and almonds. Then add enough oat flour to make a dough of a good consistency to hold together. Shape the dough into small balls, the size of a walnut. Place the balls on greased cooky sheets. Flatten each with the bottom of a glass dipped in cold water. Sprinkle the tops with cinnamon. Bake at 300° F. for 12 to 15 minutes. Yields 4 to 4½ dozen wafers.

WALNUT WAFERS

1 cup date sugar, firmly packed
1 tablespoon unsulfured molasses
2 eggs, beaten
1 cup English walnuts, ground
½ cup oat flour (about)

Blend all the ingredients together, in the order given, using only enough oat flour to form a batter that can be dropped by teaspoonfuls onto greased and floured cooky sheets. Allow space between the wafers on the cooky sheets, because they will spread. Bake at 350° F. for 8 to 10 minutes, or until brown. Remove the wafers from the sheets immediately. If the wafers stick to the cooky sheets, put them back in the warm oven for a short time, and then remove them from the sheets. Yields 2 to 2½ dozen wafers.

PEANUT WAFERS

½ cup honey
½ cup softened butter
1 cup milk
½ cup peanuts, broken
2 cups oat flour (about)

Blend all the ingredients, in the order given, using enough oat flour to make a thin batter. Pour 1-inch rounds, with spaces between for spreading, on greased, floured cooky sheets. Bake at 375° F. for 5 to 6 minutes. Remove from sheets immediately. Yields 3 dozen wafers.

VANILLA-COCONUT WAFERS

¾ cup honey
½ cup oil
3 eggs
2 tablespoons milk
1½ teaspoons vanilla extract
2¾ cups oat flour (about)
½ cup dried coconut shreds, unsweetened

Blend the honey and the oil. Add the eggs, reserving the white of one egg for later use. Add the milk, vanilla, and enough oat flour to make a firm dough. Chill. Roll out the dough to ⅛-inch thickness. Cut into 2-inch round wafers. Brush the tops of the wafers with egg white, and then sprinkle them with dried coconut shreds. Place the wafers on greased cooky sheets. Bake at 400° F. for 8 minutes. Yields 6 dozen wafers.

DATE SUGAR WAFERS

1 cup date sugar, packed firmly
½ cup oil
1 egg
¼ cup milk
2 teaspoons vanilla extract
½ cup soy flour
½ cup wheat germ
½ cup wholewheat flour (about)

Blend together the date sugar and the oil. Add the rest of the ingredients, using enough wholewheat flour to make a batter of a good consistency to drop by teaspoonfuls onto greased cooky sheets. Bake at 350° F. for 8 to 10 minutes. Yields 3 dozen wafers.

MOLASSES WAFERS

1 cup unsulfured molasses
½ cup honey
½ cup oil
1 tablespoon ginger, ground
2 cups oat flour (about)

Blend all the ingredients together, in the order listed, adding enough oat flour to make a thin dough. Drop by ½ teaspoonfuls, spaced 2½ inches apart, on greased cooky sheets. Bake at 350° F. for 10 to 12 minutes. Cool slightly, and then turn each wafer over. Roll the wafers, with the glossy side out, over the handle of a wooden spoon. If the cookies become too crisp to roll, soften them by returning them to the warm oven for a minute or two. Yields 7 dozen wafers.

SHREWSBURY WAFERS

¾ cup honey
1 cup oil
3 eggs
½ teaspoon mace, ground
3½ cups oat flour (about)

Blend all the ingredients, adding enough oat flour to make a firm dough. Chill the dough, and then roll it out to ⅛-inch thickness. Cut into 2-inch round wafers, and place the wafers on greased cooky sheets. Bake at 375° F. for 8 minutes, or until lightly browned. Yields 2 to 2½ dozen wafers.

LEMON WAFERS

½ cup softened butter
⅔ cup honey
4 eggs, beaten
2 teaspoons lemon extract
2¼ cups oat flour (about)

Blend the butter and the honey. Add the eggs and lemon extract, and mix thoroughly. Add enough flour to make a dough of a good consistency to drop by teaspoonfuls on greased cooky sheets. Allow space between the wafers, because they will spread. Bake the wafers at 350° F. for 5 to 6 minutes, or until browned lightly around the edges. Yields 4 to 5 dozen wafers.

ROLLED OAT ROCKS

1 cup maple sugar
$\frac{1}{2}$ cup oil
1 egg
5 tablespoons milk
1 teaspoon vanilla extract
$\frac{1}{2}$ teaspoon allspice, ground
$\frac{3}{4}$ teaspoon cinnamon, ground
$\frac{1}{2}$ cup dried fruit, chopped
$\frac{1}{2}$ cup nutmeats, broken
$1\frac{3}{4}$ cups rolled oats, uncooked
$1\frac{1}{2}$ cups corn flour (about)

Blend all the ingredients, in the order given, adding enough corn flour to make a dough of a good consistency to drop by teaspoonfuls onto greased cooky sheets. Bake at 375° F. for 10 to 12 minutes, or until firm in texture and slightly browned. Yields 6 dozen rocks.

APPLE-OATMEAL ROCKS

1 cup honey
½ cup oil
3 tablespoons carob powder
1 cup grated apple, raw
3 cups rolled oats, raw
1 cup nutmeats, broken
1 teaspoon vanilla extract

Place in a saucepan the honey, oil, carob powder, and apple. Boil the mixture for 1 minute. Remove the hot mixture from the heat, and pour it into a bowl. Add the oats, and blend thoroughly. Stir in the nutmeats and vanilla. Drop the mixture by heaping teaspoonfuls onto waxed paper. Chill. Yields 6 dozen rocks.

COCONUT-OATMEAL ROCKS

½ cup honey
¾ cup oil
2 cups rolled oats, uncooked
2 eggs, beaten
1 teaspoon vanilla extract
¾ cup sunflower seed meal
1 cup dried coconut shreds, unsweetened.

Blend together the honey, oil, and oats. Refrigerate this mixture for several hours. Then add the rest of the ingredients, and mix thoroughly. Drop by teaspoonfuls onto greased cooky sheets. Bake at 350° F. for 8 to 10 minutes. Yields 3 dozen rocks.

PECAN ROCKS

¼ cup sorghum syrup
¾ cup oil
2 teaspoons vanilla extract
1 cup pecans, broken
2½ cups oat flour (about)

Blend all the ingredients together, using enough oat flour to make a dough of a good consistency to hold together. Drop by teaspoonfuls onto greased cooky sheets. Bake at 300° F. for 30 to 35 minutes. Yields 5 dozen rocks.

DATE SUGAR ROCKS

¾ cup date sugar
½ cup oil
½ cup milk
1 teaspoon vanilla extract
1 cup rolled oats, uncooked
1 cup wheat germ
½ cup nutmeats, broken
½ cup raisins, steamed
1 cup wholewheat flour (about)

Blend together the date sugar, oil, milk, and vanilla. Add to this mixture the remaining ingredients, using enough wholewheat flour to make the dough a good consistency to drop by teaspoonfuls onto greased cooky sheets. Bake at 350° F. for 12 to 15 minutes. Yields 6 dozen rocks.

HONEY-MOLASSES ROCKS

½ cup honey
½ cup unsulfured molasses
1 cup oil
1 teaspoon vanilla extract
½ cup grated orange rind, from organic fruit
1 cup soy flour
2 cups wholewheat flour (about)

Blend all the ingredients together, adding enough wholewheat flour to make the dough a good consistency to drop by teaspoonfuls onto greased cooky sheets. Bake at 350° F. for 8 to 10 minutes, or until brown. Yields 4 dozen rocks.

Crisps, Chews

PECAN CRISPS

⅔ cup honey
½ cup oil
1 egg yolk
3 tablespoons milk
1 teaspoon vanilla extract
1½ cups oat flour (about)
1 egg white
½ cup pecans, broken

Blend together, in the order listed, the honey, oil, egg yolk, milk, and vanilla. Add to this mixture enough oat flour to make a dough of a good consistency to hold together. Chill. Shape the dough into small balls, the size of a walnut. Place the balls on greased cooky sheets, and flatten each with the bottom of a glass dipped in cold water. Brush the tops with egg white, and then sprinkle with the pecans. Bake at 375° F. for 8 to 10 minutes, or until lightly browned. Yields 5 dozen crisps.

CARAWAY CRISPS

1 cup honey
1 cup softened butter
2 eggs
2 tablespoons buttermilk
1 tablespoon caraway seeds, ground
3 cups oat flour (about)

Blend the honey and the butter. Add the eggs, one at a time, beating the mixture thoroughly after each addition. Add the buttermilk and caraway seeds. Then add enough oat flour to make a dough of a good consistency to hold together. Chill. Roll out to ¼-inch thickness, and cut with a cooky cutter. Place on greased cooky sheets. Bake at 350° F. for 15 to 20 minutes. Yields 6 dozen crisps.

SOYBEAN CRISPS

2 cups date sugar, firmly packed
3 tablespoons oil
3 tablespoons water
1 cup toasted soybeans, ground*
1 cup oat flour (about)

Blend all the ingredients thoroughly, adding enough oat flour to make a dough of a good consistency to drop by teaspoonfuls onto greased cooky sheets. Bake at 300° F. for 8 to 10 minutes, or until brown. Remove from the sheets at once. Yields 6 dozen crisps.

* To toast soybeans, begin by soaking a cup of soybeans overnight in 4 cups of cold water. In the morning, drain the soybeans, and spread them out on a shallow pan. Place them in an oven set at 200° F., and allow them to dry out for about 2 hours. Then place the soybeans directly under the broiler. As they broil, shake them constantly to brown them evenly. Allow them to cool. Then grind them in an electric seed grinder, or crush them with a mortar and pestle.

MOLASSES CRISPS

¾ cup unsulfured molasses
¼ cup blackstrap molasses
¾ cup oil
1 egg
¼ cup oat flour
¼ cup soy flour
2 cups wholewheat flour (about)

Blend all the ingredients together, adding enough wholewheat flour to make a dough of a good consistency to hold together. Shape the dough into 2 long rolls, wrap in waxed paper, and chill until firm. Cut into slices about ¼-inch thick. Place the slices on greased, floured cooky sheets. Bake at 350° F. for 8 to 10 minutes, or until brown. Yields 3 dozen crisps.

OATMEAL CHEWS

1 cup honey
1 cup oil
4 cups rolled oats, uncooked
2 eggs, beaten
1 tablespoon vanilla extract
1 cup oat flour (about)

Blend the honey, oil, and rolled oats in a bowl. Cover, and let stand overnight. In the morning, add the eggs, vanilla, and enough oat flour to make a dough of a good consistency to hold together. Roll the dough into balls, the size of a walnut. Place the balls on greased cooky sheets. Flatten each with the bottom of a glass dipped in cold water. Bake at 350° F. for 10 to 12 minutes. Remove from the cooky sheets while hot. Yields 6 dozen chews.

DATE-NUT CHEWS

½ cup date sugar, firmly packed
½ cup malt syrup
2 eggs
½ teaspoon almond extract
1 cup pitted dates, chopped
1 cup nutmeats, chopped
¾ cups oat flour (about)

Blend together all the ingredients, using enough oat flour to make a dough of a good consistency to hold together. Place the dough in 2 greased and floured 8x8x2-inch pans. Bake at 375° F. for 20 to 25 minutes. While still hot, cut into 2x2-inch squares. Yields 2⅔ dozen chews.

SESAME CHEWS

¾ cup sesame seeds
1 cup honey
2 tablespoons oil
1 egg, beaten
1 teaspoon vanilla extract
¼ cup wholewheat flour (about)
additional oil

Toast the sesame seeds by heating them, unoiled, in a skillet. Shake or stir them constantly until evenly toasted a light brown. Remove at once and cool. Blend together thoroughly the honey, oil, egg, and vanilla. Add to this mixture ½ cup of the cooled sesame seeds. Then add enough wholewheat flour to make a firm dough. Roll the dough into small balls, the size of a walnut. Dip each of the balls into oil, and then place it on a cooky sheet. Flatten the balls with the bottom of a glass dipped in cold water. Sprinkle the tops with the remaining ¼ cup of sesame seeds. Press the seeds into the balls with the bottom of a glass. Bake at 350° F. for 5 to 8 minutes. Yields 2 dozen chews.

CRUNCHY CHEWS

1 cup date sugar, firmly packed
1 cup oil
2 eggs
¼ cup milk
1 teaspoon almond extract
2 cups nutmeats, broken
2½ cups rolled oats, uncooked
½ cup wholewheat flour (about)

Blend together all the ingredients, in the order given, adding enough wholewheat flour to make a batter of a good consistency to drop by teaspoonfuls onto greased cooky sheets. Flatten each cooky with the bottom of a glass dipped in cold water. Bake at 325° F. for 8 to 10 minutes, or until brown. Yields 3 dozen chews.

Sand Tarts, Mounds Crescents, Patties, Snaps

SAND TARTS

In the days of early Christianity small heart-shaped cakes were baked on saints' days. They were called Life Cakes or Saints' Hearts. Later, these cakes were ornamented and bestowed as gifts on saints' days. The name became distorted from Saints' Hearts to Sand Tarts. The museum at Bath, England, has a collection of old cutters used in making these cakes.

1 cup honey
1 cup oil
1 teaspoon grated lemon rind, from organic fruit
3 egg whites
3½ cups oat flour (about)
½ cup nutmeats, broken
cinnamon

Blend the honey, oil, lemon rind, and 2 of the egg whites. Add to this mixture enough oat flour to make a dough of a good consistency to hold together. Chill. Roll to ⅛-inch thickness, and cut into 2-inch rounds. Place the rounds on greased cooky sheets. Brush the tops with egg white, and then sprinkle with the nutmeats. Bake at 350° F. for 8 minutes. After removing the tarts from the oven, dust the tops with cinnamon. Then return the tarts to the oven for another minute. Yields 5 dozen tarts.

SAND TARTS WITH ALMONDS

⅔ cup honey
⅔ cup oil
2 eggs
1 teaspoon almond extract
4¼ cups oat flour (about)
1 cup almonds, blanched

Blend together the honey, oil, eggs, and almond extract. Add to this mixture enough oat flour to make a dough of a good consistency to hold together. Chill. Roll to ⅛-inch thickness, and cut into 2-inch round tarts. Place the tarts on greased cooky sheets. Press into each tart a blanched almond. Bake the tarts at 375° F. for 8 to 10 minutes, or until golden brown. Yields 5 to 5½ dozen tarts.

COCONUT MOUNDS

¾ cup date sugar, packed firmly
⅓ cup oil
1 egg, beaten
⅓ cup milk
1 teaspoon vanilla extract
½ teaspoon cinnamon, ground
1 cup dried coconut shreds, unsweetened
2 cups oat flour (about)

Blend all the ingredients together, in the order given, using only enough oat flour to make a dough of a good consistency to drop by teaspoonfuls onto greased cooky sheets. Bake at 350° F. for 8 to 10 minutes. Yields 3 to 3½ dozen mounds.

ALMOND CRESCENTS

1 cup softened butter
⅓ cup honey
2 teaspoons water
2 teaspoons vanilla extract
2 cups oat flour (about)
melted butter
½ cup almonds, ground

Blend together the butter and the honey. Add to this blend the water and vanilla, and mix thoroughly. Then add enough flour to make a dough of a good consistency to hold together. Chill the dough for a few hours. Then shape it into long rolls, about 1 inch in diameter. Cut off 3-inch strips, and shape into crescents. Brush the tops with melted butter, and sprinkle with almonds. Place the crescents on ungreased cooky sheets. Bake at 325° F. for 10 to 15 minutes. Yields 3 to 3½ dozen crescents.

GOLDEN CRESCENTS

½ cup honey
½ cup softened butter
4 hard-cooked egg yolks, mashed
2 teaspoons grated orange rind, from organic fruit
¼ cup English walnuts, ground
¾ cup oat flour (about)

Blend all the ingredients together, in the order given, using enough oat flour to make a dough of a good consistency to hold together. Chill the dough. Then shape it into long rolls, about 1 inch in diameter. Cut off 3-inch pieces and shape them into crescents. Place the crescents on greased cooky sheets. Bake at 350° F. for 10 to 12 minutes. Yields 2½ to 3 dozen crescents.

DATE-ALMOND PATTIES

½ cup date sugar, firmly packed
½ cup honey
½ cup oil
⅔ cup pitted dates, ground
½ cup milk
1 cup almonds, ground
1½ cups rolled oats, uncooked
1 cup wheat germ
2 teaspoons vanilla extract
½ cup oat flour (about)

Blend together all the ingredients, in the order given, using enough oat flour to make a dough of a good consistency to hold together. Chill the dough. Then shape it into balls, the size of a plum. Place the balls on greased cooky sheets, and flatten each with the bottom of a glass dipped in cold water. Bake at 350° F. for 10 to 12 minutes. Yields 5 to 6 dozen patties.

GINGER SNAPS

- ¾ cup honey
- ¾ cup unsulfured molasses
- ¼ cup blackstrap molasses
- 1 egg
- 1 tablespoon vinegar
- 4 teaspoons ginger, ground
- 4 cups oat flour (about)

Blend all the ingredients together, in the order given, using enough oat flour to make a firm dough. Roll out the dough to ⅛-inch thickness, and cut into 2-inch rounds. Place the rounds on greased cooky sheets. Bake at 350° F. for 8 minutes. Yields 6 dozen snaps.

Macaroons, Kisses

OATMEAL MACAROONS

2 egg whites
2 cups maple sugar
2 cups rolled oats, uncooked
1 teaspoon vanilla extract
½ cup dried coconut shreds, unsweetened

Beat the egg whites until stiff. Gradually add the maple sugar, and continue beating until very stiff. Add to this mixture the remaining ingredients, and mix thoroughly. Drop by teaspoonfuls onto greased and floured cooky sheets. Bake at 350° F. for 10 to 12 minutes. Allow the macaroons to cool on the cooky sheets. Yields 3 dozen macaroons.

DATE-COCONUT MACAROONS

4 egg whites
1¼ cups honey
1 teaspoon vanilla extract
2 cups pitted dates, chopped
2⅔ cups dried coconut shreds, unsweetened

Beat the egg whites until stiff. Gradually add the honey, and continue beating until very stiff. Add the remaining ingredients, and mix thoroughly. Drop by teaspoonfuls onto greased and floured cooky sheets. Bake at 275° F. for 20 to 25 minutes. Allow the macaroons to cool on the cooky sheets. Yields 3½ to 4 dozen macaroons.

ALMOND MACAROONS

4 egg whites
1½ cups honey
1 teaspoon almond extract
1½ cups blanched almonds, ground

Beat the egg whites until stiff. Gradually add the honey, and continue beating until very stiff. Blend in the almond extract and the almonds. Drop by teaspoonfuls onto greased and floured cooky sheets. Bake at 350° F. for 15 to 20 minutes, or until lightly browned. Allow the macaroons to cool on the cooky sheets. Yields 3 dozen macaroons.

COCONUT-NUT MACAROONS

- 4 egg whites
- 1⅓ cups date sugar, firmly packed
- ⅔ cup honey
- 2 cups dried coconut shreds, unsweetened
- 2 cups pitted dates, ground
- 4 cups nutmeats, ground

Beat the egg whites until stiff. Gradually add the date sugar and honey, and continue beating until very stiff. Mix in the rest of the ingredients. Drop by teaspoonfuls onto greased and floured cooky sheets. Bake at 350° F. for 15 to 20 minutes, or until lightly browned. Allow the macaroons to cool on the cooky sheets. Yields 8 dozen macaroons.

SUNFLOWER SEED KISSES

6 egg whites
1⅓ cups date sugar, firmly packed
1 teaspoon lemon extract
1⅓ cups sunflower seed meal

Beat the egg whites until stiff. Gradually add the date sugar, and continue beating until very stiff. Blend in the lemon extract and the sunflower seed meal. Drop by teaspoonfuls onto greased and floured cooky sheets. Bake at 300° F. for 15 to 20 minutes. Allow the kisses to cool on the cooky sheets. Yields 4 dozen kisses.

FILBERT KISSES

8 egg whites
1½ cups honey
1 teaspoon vanilla extract
2¾ cups filberts, ground

Beat the egg whites until stiff. Gradually add the honey, and continue beating until very stiff. Blend in the vanilla and filberts. Drop by teaspoonfuls onto greased and floured cooky sheets. Bake at 300° F. for 15 to 20 minutes. Allow the kisses to cool on the cooky sheets. Yields 5 dozen kisses.

COCONUT KISSES

6 egg whites
½ cup honey
1 teaspoon vanilla extract
3 cups dried coconut shreds, unsweetened

Beat the egg whites until stiff. Gradually add the honey, and continue beating until very stiff. Blend in the vanilla and coconut shreds. Drop by teaspoonfuls onto greased and floured cooky sheets. Bake at 300° F. for 15 to 20 minutes. Allow the kisses to cool on the cooky sheets. Yields 4 dozen kisses.

*Confections Without Objections**

* Eaten in moderation and followed by an apple!

POPCORN CONFECTION

1 cup unsulfured molasses
⅓ cup honey
6 cups popped corn
2 cups peanuts

Place the molasses and the honey in a saucepan, and boil the mixture until it threads. Mix the popcorn and peanuts together, and turn them into a greased 12x8x2-inch pan. Pour the syrup mixture over them, and allow the confection to cool.

CAROB CONFECTION

1½ cups date sugar, firmly packed
⅓ cup carob syrup
⅓ cup whey powder
⅓ cup carob powder
1 tablespoon oil
½ cup sesame seeds

Place in a saucepan the date sugar, carob syrup, whey powder, carob powder, and oil. Blend the mixture thoroughly. Heat gently, bring to a simmer, stir constantly, and continue to cook gently. Remove from the heat when a teaspoonful of the mixture forms a ball when dropped into cold water. Turn the mixture into a greased, floured 12x8x1-inch pan. Sprinkle the top with sesame seeds. Chill. Cut into 1x1-inch squares. Yields 8 dozen confections.

MAPLE SYRUP CONFECTION

2 cups maple syrup
1 cup heavy cream

Blend the 2 ingredients together in a saucepan, and heat gently. Stir constantly, and continue cooking until a thread forms, at 234° F. Remove the mixture from the heat, and beat until thick and creamy. Drop by teaspoonfuls onto greased cooky sheets, allowing space between. Refrigerate. When the confections have cooled and hardened, wrap each individually in waxed paper. Yields 10 dozen small confections.

POPPY SEED CONFECTION

2 cups honey
½ cup maple sugar
2 pounds poppy seeds
2 cups filberts, ground

Combine the honey, sugar, and poppy seeds in a saucepan. Cook the mixture over a low heat, stirring frequently, for about 30 minutes, or until it thickens. Add the filberts, and mix thoroughly. Turn into 2 greased and floured 8x8x2-inch pans. Refrigerate until cool and hardened. Since this is a confection, pieces can be cut quite small. Cut into 1x1-inch squares, and wrap each individually in waxed paper. Refrigerate. Yields 8⅔ dozen confections.

FRUIT-NUT ROLLS

3 cups honey
1 cup milk
1 cup dried unsulfured apricots, chopped
1 cup pitted dates, chopped
1 cup nutmeats, chopped
1 teaspoon almond extract

Place the honey and the milk in a saucepan. Bring to a boil over a gentle heat. Add the fruits, and continue to cook over a low heat until the mixture forms a soft, firm ball when a teaspoonful of it is dropped into cold water. Remove the mixture from the heat, and add the nuts and almond extract. Beat until stiff. Shape into 2 12-inch-long rolls, and wrap in waxed paper. Refrigerate. Slice into ¼-inch pieces. Yields 8 dozen slices.

UNCOOKED TOOTSIE ROLLS

½ cup honey
½ cup date sugar, firmly packed
1 cup carob powder
1 cup wheat germ
½ cup soy grits
1 cup soy lecithin granules
1 cup dried coconut shreds, unsweetened
½ cup oil
2 teaspoons vanilla extract
1 cup sunflower seed meal
water

Blend all the ingredients together thoroughly, using enough water to make a dough of a good consistency to hold together. Divide the dough into thirds, shape into 3 18-inch-long flat rolls, and refrigerate overnight. Cut into slices ½-inch thick, and wrap individually in waxed paper. Refrigerate. Yields 9 dozen tootsie rolls.

UNCOOKED MOCK FUDGE

1 cup honey
½ cup oil
⅔ cup carob powder
4 cups nonfat dry milk powder
2 cups English walnuts, broken
milk

Blend together the honey, oil, carob powder, milk powder, and walnuts. Add to this blend only enough milk to make a mixture of a good consistency to hold together. Pat into a greased 12x8x2-inch pan. Chill. Since this is a confection, it can be cut in very small pieces. Cut into 1x1-inch squares, and wrap each individually in waxed paper. Refrigerate or freeze. Yields 8 dozen confections.

FRUIT-NUT DANDIES

1 cup maple sugar
½ cup water
1 cup dried fruits, chopped
½ cup nutmeats, chopped

Boil together the maple sugar and the water until the syrup forms a soft ball in cold water. Add the fruits and nutmeats. Mix thoroughly. Drop by teaspoonfuls onto greased plates, allowing ½-inch spaces between the dandies. Allow to cool. Refrigerate. Yields 3 to 3½ dozen dandies.

UNCOOKED PEANUT BUTTER CONFECTION

1 cup honey
1 cup peanut butter
2 cups nonfat dry milk powder (about)

Blend together all the ingredients listed, using enough dry milk powder to make a dough of a good consistency to hold together. Shape the dough into 1 12-inch-long roll, wrap in waxed paper, and refrigerate. Cut into $\frac{1}{4}$-inch slices, and wrap each individually in waxed paper. Refrigerate or freeze. Yields 4 dozen confections.

FROZEN BANANA SURPRISE
(in blender)

3 cups water
3 bananas, fully ripe
6 tablespoons whey powder
1 tablespoon brewer's yeast
¼ cup honey
½ cup nutmeats, broken

Blend all the ingredients together in an electric blender, and turn the mixture into ice cube trays. Replace the cube dividers and freeze. Remove, and wrap individually in waxed paper. Return to freezer. Yields about 3½ dozen cubes.

HALVAH

This delicious Near East confection, uncooked, is traditionally made with honey and tahini. Tahini is sesame seeds, ground finely, like peanut butter. It can be obtained from health food stores, and mail order companies selling health foods.

1 cup honey
1½ cups tahini
2 cups nonfat dry milk powder
½ cup whey powder
½ cup carob powder

Blend all the ingredients together thoroughly, and turn the mixture out into a greased 12x8x2-inch pan. Chill, and allow to become firm. Since halvah is a confection, pieces can be cut quite small. Cut into 1x1-inch squares, and wrap each individually in waxed paper. Refrigerate. Yields 8 dozen confections.

Index

Index

Index